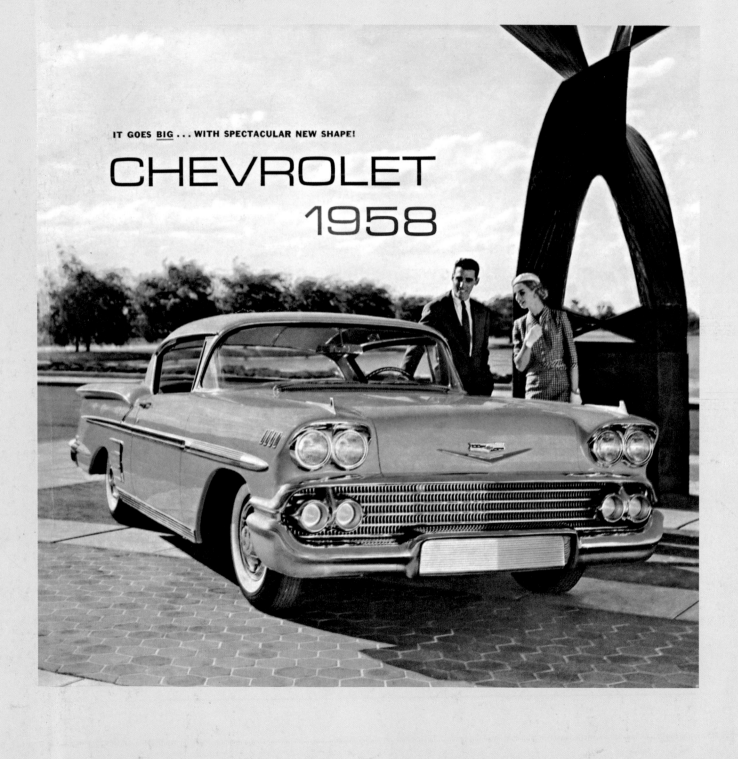

IT GOES BIG . . . WITH SPECTACULAR NEW SHAPE!

CHEVROLET
1958

ROAD HOGS

ONE OF 3 SENSIBLE SPECTACULARS—1965 RAMBLER AMBASSADOR
...largest and finest of the new RAMBLERS

Detroit's Big, Beautiful Luxury Performance Cars of the 1960s

ERIC PETERS

motorbooks

First published in 2011 by MBI Publishing Company LLC and Motorbooks, an imprint of MBI Publishing Company, 400 First Avenue North, Suite 300, Minneapolis, MN, 55401 USA

The information in this book is true and complete to the best of our knowledge. All recommendations are made without any guarantee on the part of the author or Publisher, who also disclaim any liability incurred in connection with the use of this data or specific details.

We recognize that some words, model names, and designations mentioned herein are the property of the trademark holder. We use them for identification purposes only. This is not an official publication.

MBI Publishing Company titles are also available at discounts in bulk quantity for industrial or sales-promotional use. For details write to Special Sales Manager at MBI Publishing Company, 400 First Avenue North, Suite 300, Minneapolis, MN, 55401 USA

Library of Congress Cataloging-in-Publication Data

Peters, Eric (Eric Christopher)
 Road hogs : Detroit's big, beautiful luxury performance cars of the 1960s and 1970s / Eric Peters.
    p. cm.
 ISBN-13: 978-0-7603-3764-6
 ISBN-10: 0-7603-3388-2
 1. Automobiles—United States—History—20th century. 2. Muscle cars—United States—History—20th century. 3. Antique and classic cars—United States. I. Title.
 TL23.P48 2011
 629.222—dc22

                                                                2009031131

Printed in China

On the front cover: Photo © Dan Lyons

On the back cover: Cadillac Coupe DeVille, from the Barney Olson collection

On the frontis: Shutterstock

On the title pages: The cover of Chevrolet's 1958 brochure and the cover of American Motor Corporation's 1965 Rambler Ambassador brochure. *Barney Olson collection*

Photo Credits
All images from the Byron Olson collection, with the exception of the following:
Everett Collection, pp. 14, 90;
Shutterstock, pp. 15, 17, 37, 48, 57, 83, 84–85, 110–111, 118, 123, 126–127;
© Performance Image/Alamy, pp. 32–33, 101, 124, 126 bottom;
© Motoring Picture Library/Alamy, pp. 43, 72–73, 121;
© Phil Talbot/Alamy, pp. 47, 122;
iStockphoto, pp. 54, 95, 114;
© Ken Stepnell/Photolibrary, p. 81;
© Oleksiy Maksymenko/Alamy, p. 125;
© Alan Stone/Alamy, p. 150.
© Dan Lyons, p. 7, 8–9, 13, 134–135, 141–142, 142, 143, 154–155, 155.

CONTENTS

INTRODUCTION

You'll sometimes read about old folks who can remember what the world was like before there were cars at all. Someday, I will be like them—only my memories will be of a time, briefly glimpsed and long gone, when footloose flotillas of enormous land yachts surfed the roads, free of care about their carbon footprint or their gas mileage. Great glitzy ingots of excess, whitewall tired and landau roofed—their mighty prows bedecked in chrome, their flanks adorned with inscriptions that read *d'Elegance* and *Brougham*. No sad-sack alphanumeric designations: These were cars deserving not merely of names, but *titles*.

Try to imagine a two-door "personal" coupe with room for six 200-pound adults and a trunk with more square footage than a typical home bathtub/shower combo. This was a time when virtually every car on the road was Made in the U.S.A. and carried a huge V-8 under its hood—all that gloriously gratuitous excess power flowing to the rear wheels, unimpeded by traction control, ABS, or any sort of Big Momma electronic nanny. I sometimes have vivid, personal flashbacks of What It Was Like . . .

As a kid in the '70s, my parents owned a monstrous bile-green Oldsmobile 98 Regency sedan. I remember the Tiffany clock in the dash, the plush-pile carpet, the acres of backseat space.

And, of course, the speed.

My mother would blast down the Merritt Parkway on the way to New York City, at 80 or 90 miles per hour, the big beast bullying along powerfully, like a steamship with its boilers fully fired and all three screws churning the seas.

In the back, you could hunker down and put your head against the carpeted floor and feel the soothing drone of the road, the warmth of the Rocket 455's exhaust pulses penetrating through the insulation. There were no DVD entertainment systems, juice box holders, or child safety seats. We made our own entertainment and, besides, the grown-ups were far away up front—for all practical purposes, in another zip code.

When, a few years later, the time came to learn how to drive, we lucky children of the '60s and '70s did so not behind the wheel of browbeaten front drive economy cars but in full command of rear-drive road titans without any of the crutches—or precision—of modern cars. You learned to deal with feather-light and over-boosted power steering, non-ABS (and completely marginal) brakes, oppressed 70-series radials and their propensity to throw off wheel covers during hard lean. It was easy enough to get into trouble but hard to get hurt because of the sheer massiveness of your steed. You grew to be a better wheelman as a result, though. Drive one of these things well and you can drive anything.

Few things can rise to the occasion like doing an open-axled, single-tire burnout in a fender-skirted Olds with a seven-liter V-8 under the hood.

For adults, meanwhile, it was a kinder, gentler era.

The heavy cruisers of the 1960s and early to mid-1970s defined luxury differently than it's taken to mean today—when even big sedans try desperately to be sporty—from their individual bucket seats to their console-shifted transmissions.

Yes, they are fast and handle and are capable of many things the old tanks could never hope to manage—but then, that wasn't what the Old Beasts were all about. Until you have spread yourself out across the bouncy bench seat of an undefiled, undiluted, Grade A American Road Hog, pulled the column-shifted automatic into Drive, looked across that flight deck expanse of hood—and felt the entire front end rise up on its shocks as you ease into the throttle—you will simply never get it.

This book will try to fill in the gaps for those who missed it all—and provide a trip down Memory Lane for those who didn't . . . and sorely miss it.

Like real fireworks that explode and fly—and guns you can buy without ID through the mail and flying on an airplane without showing ID and paying cash for your ticket—they are totems of a different America. A time fast fading in the rearview mirror. It is almost hard to believe such things were once as commonplace as pull-top soda cans.

And now, gone forever.

If a buyer wanted to really mix his or her metaphors, he or she could order a Continental kit for his or her Caddy.

Cadillac Eldorado
Pontiac Catalina
Pontiac GrandVille
Chrysler 300 convertible
Ford Galaxie 500/XL/LTD convertible

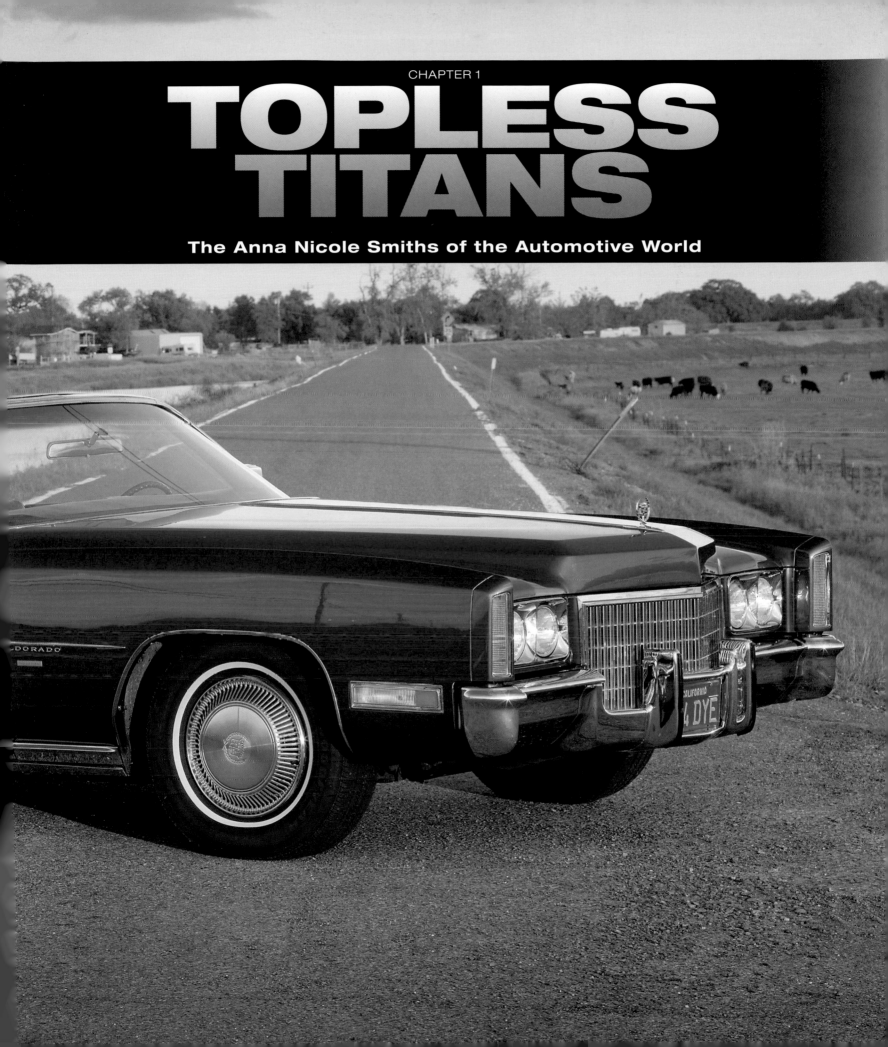

CHAPTER 1

TOPLESS TITANS

The Anna Nicole Smiths of the Automotive World

PRESENTING

THE *Cadillac* ELDORADO

El Dorado, a city of gold that was rumored to exist in South America, long attracted adventure seekers, such as Sir Walter Raleigh. None of those seekers ever found such a place, though if they had, chances are it wouldn't have been as opulent as Cadillac's Eldorado model, introduced for the 1953 model year.

Previous pages: **In 1971** nothing said you'd arrived like arriving in a Cadillac Eldorado. ©*Ron Kimball/ Kimball Stock*

CAVERNOUS
CADILLAC
ELDORADO
1953-1955

Cadillac has always been General Motors' luxury division—and remains so to this day, even though it's been developing a reputation for performance in recent years. But the Cadillac of yesterday was a very different company in a very different time.

Before there was such a thing as a Japanese luxury car, when BMW and Mercedes were minor irritants, Cadillac was indeed the "standard of the world" and its land yachts prowled the roads like nothing before or since.

They were huge and intimidating, the favored conveyances of Texas cattlemen, movie stars—anyone with real money and not afraid to let the world know about it.

At high tide, in the fullness of their glory, the biggest of them stretched 20 feet from bumperette to fin tip—and were propelled by V-8 engines with pistons the diameter of Maxwell House coffee cans. In some models, speedometers spread across the dashboard, the fonts canting rightward like a pre-digital warp-speed indicator as the numbers rose ever higher . . . 80, 90, 110 miles per hour.

From 1953 until 1955, the Eldorado was only offered as a convertible, but in 1956, Cadillac offered it in either convertible (*Biarritz* in Cadillac-speak) or coupe (*Seville*) form. For 1956, Cadillac also bumped the displacement of its V-8 engine to 365 cubic inches. In the Eldorado, this translated to 305 horsepower, which was 20 horsepower more than in more pedestrian Cadillac models.

Only from the great traditions of Cadillac could there come a motor car as surpassingly fine as that portrayed below—the 1959 Eldorado Biarritz. Luxurious beyond description, it offers spectacular performance and handling ease. Every known motoring advancement makes each journey memorable. Standard equipment includes a custom engineered 345-horsepower engine, air suspension, electrically powered front seat adjustment, electric door locks and window regulators, power steering and braking, radio and heater. Interiors are offered in deep-grained Cardiff and Florentine leathers in tones of bronze metallic ... blue metallic ... gray metallic ... slate green metallic ... black ... white ... and red.

THE NEW STANDARD OF THE WORLD IN SPLENDOR!

ELDORADO BIARRITZ

As the 1950s wound to a close, the tailfin craze had overshot its zenith, and fins had grown to gargantuan proportions, but none were more excessive than those found on the 1959 Cadillac Eldorado.

It was a time when it was considered bad form not to consume at least three martinis over lunch, pregnant women smoked, no one cared about their cholesterol level—let alone global warming or their carbon footprint. Audaciousness and comfort sold cars—and Cadillac was the acknowledged master of both.

A good name is a good beginning—and when Cadillac decided to christen its ultra-convertible after the mythical "gilded one" of Aztec/Mayan legend, it could not have chosen a more fitting nom de plume.

The Eldorado was over the top from Day One—an unapologetic expression of American postwar supremacy—a stamped-steel reminder of GM's status as the world's mightiest industrial colossus.

Harkening back to the coach-built era of the 1920s and 1930s, the very first production Eldorado was a low-volume, custom-bodied (and essentially hand-built) production version of the El Dorado show car first displayed at the GM Motorama in 1952. It rode on a modified version of the Series 62 coupe's chassis, extended to a palatial 221 inches. Overall length would reach to the ends of the earth by the following year, when the Eldo got stretched to a fulsome 223.4 inches—about eighteen and a half feet of wire-wheeled, zoot-suited extravagance.

Amazingly, even bigger things were yet to come.

GM's legendary styling chief, Harley Earl, was the man primarily responsible for the look of this imposing machine, of which just 532 examples (according to GM

records) were made. All of them were convertibles (in 1956, a hardtop Seville version would be added to the lineup), with a special all-metal tonneau cover shared with no other General Motors vehicle.

The first-year Eldo rode low and wide on real wire wheels and double fat whitewall tires—the rears fully skirted in the fashion of the times. A vast panoramic wraparound windshield just like the one found on the El Dorado show car gave the driver unimpaired forward and peripheral views. Up front, heavy-lidded headlights and a grinning gangster grille slathered in chrome, with protuberant "bullet points" on either side of

By 1955 Cadillac's Eldorado had established itself as the most lusted-after car on Earth. *Dan Lyons*

Though the output of its once-mighty 500-cubic-inch V-8 would drop to a ludicrous 190 horsepower, the Eldorado convertible was still one horny beast. And anyway, the big Cadillac was about style, not raw power.

that toothsome, mechanically menacing smile, seemed to dare jaywalkers to take the risk: Do you feel lucky?

Under the hood burbled Caddy's fully modern 331-cubic-inch OHV V-8, good for 210 horsepower. This engine weighed considerably less than its prewar forbears and was designed for high compression and high performance. (Mostly stock versions did well in racing, including the 24 Hours of Le Mans.)

Gold-plated touches adorned the car, inside and out—including the Caddy wreath and crest on the nose and the Eldorado nameplate on the dash. Even the engine was painted Cadillac gold.

The '53 Eldo's price tag was just as impressive as the car itself—$7,500 in pre-inflated, Eisenhower-era dollars. This was almost twice as much as a standard Series 62 Coupe DeVille—and was comparable to the cost of a new single family home in the 'burbs.

But then, making money off these first-year Eldorados was never the primary object for GM. The car was born to flaunt GM's might—and to herald Cadillac's stylistic dominance. It was a shot across the proverbial bow, to let others (specifically, crosstown rivals Lincoln and Chrysler) know that Caddy would brook no challengers.

In 1954, Caddy redesigned the Eldo to make it somewhat more mass-production friendly. Most of the exterior sheet metal was now shared with the Series 62 coupes and convertibles—and the sticker price was reduced to a more manageable $5,738—still a princely sum, but accessible enough that 2,150 buyers were in a position to ante up.

Power was upped, too.

For 1954, the 331 V-8's output was increased to 230 horsepower; it was soon up to 270—thanks to standard dual four-barrel carburetors (these were optional on other Cadillacs).

By 1956, the Caddy V-8 had been punched out to 365 cubic inches and was making 305 horsepower in the Eldo.

Neither GM nor Mr. Earl—the George Patton of automotive stylists—was content to let the Eldo rest on its laurels, however. In 1957, all the stops were pulled with the release of the Eldorado Brougham, a stainless-steel-roofed, suicide-doored Mafioso Mobile with a sticker price of more than $13,000—the equivalent of $100,000 in 2009 dollars.

This was the only time an Eldorado was sold as both a coupe and a four-door (pillarless) sedan.

The Brougham featured an air suspension, power seats with memory function (50 years before this feature became commonplace), an automatic trunk closer, and an Autronic Eye headlight system that automatically dimmed the high beams for oncoming cars. The 365-cubic-inch V-8 was standard—now producing 325 horsepower.

The unusual—and complex—air suspension system drew outside air into an onboard compressor that inflated rubber "air domes" at each corner of the car. These air domes were regulated by a series of valves and solenoids in order to raise or lower each corner of the car to adjust ride quality for driving conditions.

By 1965, the Eldorado was really just a fancy trim package for the DeVille convertible. Cadillac didn't develop the car during the mid-1960s because the company was preparing to launch an entirely new Eldorado for the 1967 model year.

It was a precursor to modern systems that do the same thing, but without the benefit of modern computer-controlled technology. The Eldorado Brougham's system gave Cadillac bragging rights, but gave customers headaches. Leaks and other failures were common. Many owners elected to have their cars retrofitted with conventional coil springs and hydraulic shock absorbers—and by 1960, GM dropped the air suspension system in favor of more conventional—and reliable—technology.

Models from 1959 and 1960 received revised bodywork—including most notably the jaunty tail fins that even today remain seared in the public consciousness as the apogee of American automotive glory.

Elvis drove one—and gave one to his mother, too.

A new, larger 390-cubic-inch V-8 appeared for the '59 model year, rated for 345 horsepower in the Eldorado (325 horsepower in lesser models).

Just over 900 of these ultra-extravagant, uber-Eldorados were assembled over the three-year production run, which ended in 1960.

Harley Earl retired in 1958—but his protégé Bill Mitchell would prove up to the task of keeping Caddy (and the Eldorado) on the cutting edge of automotive insolence.

The year 1961 ushered in a more restrained look, with the fins still there but toned down a bit. They would continue to shrink into the flanks through 1966, by which time they had been almost completely integrated into the side panels of the car. Upright, stacked quad headlights appeared in 1965, and the updated 390 V-8 was considered the equal or better of Rolls-Royce's powerplants of the time for high-speed smoothness.

In 1967, the Eldo that some call the Frank Sinatra Special made its debut. It was cool and suave where previous Eldorados had been swivel-hipped and duck-tailed. A vast expanse of sheet metal projected the front end into the next county well before the rest of the car arrived. A jaunty arch pressed into the sheet metal just behind the doors

When the all-new Eldorado appeared for the 1967 model year, a convertible version was not offered. Cadillac rectified this situation for the 1971 model year and reintroduced the ragtop version of this most luxurious of luxury two-doors.

The Eldorado Convertible LAST OF THE BREED.

This is more than one of the finest convertibles ever built. It is the only convertible now built in America—and it will not be repeated in 1977. You could say that Cadillac saved the best till last . . . because this is a magnificent automobile. With its ingenious inward-folding top that provides full-width seating for rear passengers. With its unique combination of front-wheel drive and four-wheel disc brakes. With a host of standard features that include an AM/FM Signal-Seeking Stereo Radio, Automatic Climate Control and Automatic Level Control.

gave the rear quarters a distinctive flair—and for the first time, the rear wheelwells were not shrouded. The wheels, meanwhile, were no longer the traditional wire-spoked design. Mag-type turbine covers—shod with thin-line whitewall tires—added a touch of sportiness.

Early cars also had hidden headlights—with vacuum-actuated retractable doors. These went away in 1969.

It was formal and very elegant-looking but more youthful and enthusiast-driver oriented. You could still cruise—but now it was also possible to bruise.

Many consider the '67 Eldorado to be one of stylist Bill Mitchell's masterpieces.

Underneath the enormous flight deck of a hood resided a 429 (and later 472) cubic-inch V-8 driving the front wheels through a specially modified, chain-drive Turbo-Hydramatic three-speed automatic transmission. It shared its basic chassis with the Oldsmobile Toronado, which had been launched the previous year—though the Olds version had its own Olds-specific engines.

The '67 front-wheel-drive Eldorado was a historic milestone for Cadillac that in many ways—both stylistically and functionally—recalled the Cord 810 of the Art Deco period more than 30 years earlier.

Front-wheel drive and 340 horsepower (375 with the larger 472) made for all sorts of fun when the gas pedal was floored. You haven't lived until you've experienced the pre-computer/pre-traction control vicious left-right pull of a 4,500-pound front-wheel-drive car with an eight-liter V-8 flexing its muscles under hard acceleration—tires squealing furiously as the driver fights to keep the prow pointed straight ahead.

Or at least, keep the thing out of the ditch.

By 1970, the Eldo was packing 500 cubic inches—8.2 liters of cast-iron Detroit Motor

By 1976, Cadillac's Eldorado was the last American convertible still in production. Cadillac marketed this fact by touting the convertible Eldo as a "last edition," but it turned out that it wouldn't be the last American convertible. It wouldn't even be the last Cadillac Eldorado convertible. Topless cars would make a comeback in the 1980s.

City V-8. It was the largest engine Cadillac (or any American automaker) would ever make and in peak tune (1970) developed 400 horsepower and an astounding 550 lb-ft of torque. This would decline, along with the power output of all GM engines, after the 1970 model year. By 1976—the final year for the 500—rated output was down to just 215 horsepower.

But in 1970, the 500-inch Eldo was truly king of the hill.

One thing was missing, though. When the '67s appeared, there was no longer a convertible in the lineup. Eldos from 1967 to 1970 were hardtop coupes only.

Buyers could at least order a power-actuated sunroof.

In 1971, the convertible option reappeared. So did another few inches of length as well as a couple hundred pounds of sheetmetal cellulite, much of it due to the need to make the big Caddy compliant with Uncle Sam's new bumper-impact requirements.

The last of the "real" Eldos strode the earth on a 126.3-inch wheelbase and (in convertible form) oppressed the scales at 4,730 pounds. Fender skirts and slab-sided fuselage styling also reappeared—marking a trend away from the sporty appearance of the 1967–1970 models and a return to the heavy cruiser look of the 1950s–1960s Eldorados.

Wise buyers sniffed change in the air and snapped up their big-cube ragtop land yachts while they still could. The year 1976 would be the final year for the convertible as well as the 500-cubic-inch V-8. There was a speculation frenzy over these supposedly "final" convertibles—of which 14,000 were eventually built, with the last 200 off the line decked out in red, white, and blue pinstriped bicentennial trim. Dealer gouging of customers interested in these cars was legendary—with some buyers reportedly paying twice the sticker price of $11,049.

Though the trimmed-down '77 and '78 Eldorados came only as hardtop coupes, they were at least still sizable compared with the rest of Detroit's offerings—outside as well as under the hood. While the 500 V-8 was gone, Caddy came through with a 425 V-8 and a gaudy Biarritz luxury package that included a thick-padded vinyl roof with opera lights on the C-pillars, two-tone paint treatments, stainless-steel trim plates, and crushed velour (or leather) seats.

Open rear wheelwells reappeared, too.

A restyled notchback Eldorado appeared for 1979—and this body style carried through to 1985. While shorter, smaller, and much lighter (by almost 1,000 pounds) than before, these were still handsome—and respectably broad-shouldered carriers of the Eldorado tradition.

A 368-cubic-inch V-8 survived through 1979–1981—still bigger than most anyone else was offering at the time. The trademark long hood survived, too. Cadillac even briefly reintroduced a convertible Eldorado for the 1984 run—although owners of the supposedly last '76 convertibles were none-too-happy about this development, having paid huge markups on their cars.

Only about 3,000 of these latter-day convertible Eldorados were made, according to records.

Though the Eldorado name lasted another 17 years, all the way to 2002, the models built from 1986 up are downsized, subdued-looking critters in comparison with their fabulous forbears. In 1987, the Allante became the star Caddy roadster—though it was destined to have a short life due to its combination of exorbitant price and poor build quality. The 1994–2002 Eldorado was a decent attempt but never had the outsized personality of the classic-era versions.

Today these latter-day shadows of the Eldorado's better days languish on used car lots at used Corolla prices—while the titans of the Earl and Mitchell eras of decades past have become highly esteemed collectibles.

ELDORADO BIARRITZ CONVERTIBLE

The Cadillac of convertibles is here! The Cadillac Eldorado Convertible. And it's everything you'd expect in a convertible that carries the Cadillac name. From its genuine leather seating areas to live to its undeniably smooth Cadillac ride.

Without a doubt, this is one convertible that truly brings luxury out in the open. The Eldorado Biarritz Convertible for 1984 (shown in Cotillion White with white top and Dark Carmine interior leather seating areas)

A WORD ABOUT THIS CATALOG: We have tried to make this catalog as comprehensive and factual as possible and we hope you find it helpful. However, since the time of printing, some of the information you will find here may have been updated. Also, some of the equipment shown or described throughout this

catalog is available at extra cost. Your dealer has details and, before ordering, you should ask him to bring you up to date. The right is reserved to make changes at any time, without notice, in prices, colors, materials, equipment, specifications and models. Check with your Cadillac dealer for more information.

Eldorado: Things to Know

The longest Eldorado wheelbase was 130 inches, in 1959–1962; these models were also the longest overall at 225 inches. The 1977–1978s come in second at 224 inches long overall.

Cadillac management reportedly considered naming the '67 Eldorado "LaSalle."

An Eldorado convertible paced the 1973 Indy 500 race. Approximately 503 pace car replicas were sold to the general public.

In the mid-1980s, GM was slapped with a class-action lawsuit over the reappearance of a convertible Eldorado in 1984–1985. Owners of '76 convertibles—which GM had aggressively marketed as the last of the Eldorado convertibles—felt the value of their convertibles as collectibles had been undermined by GM's decision to reintroduce a convertible Eldorado. GM successfully fended off the lawsuit.

Through the 1970s Cadillac outsold Lincoln, its nearest rival, by more than 3–1.

After marketing the 1976 Eldorado convertible as the "last American convertible," Cadillac infuriated collectors who had bought that car by introducing a Biarritz convertible version of the 1984 Eldorado. Fortunately, the convertible Eldorado was not available with the hellishly awful Oldsmobile diesel engine offered in Eldorado coupes.

WELL-PADDED PONCHO
PONTIAC CATALINA
1965-1972

CATALINA CONVERTIBLE

'71 Catalina

We confidently claim the new 1971 Catalina as the value leader among full-sized American cars.

It's hard to believe that Catalina's great features aren't the proud possession of many more expensive cars.

The dramatically convex sides would certainly be welcome. As would be the new grille and rugged front bumper.

The seats are a revolutionary new design with integrally molded front cushions and backs of solid foam over steel.

On top of all this soft padding you'll find either a heavily embossed brocade trimmed with Morrokide, or fully expanded Morrokide. It depends on which of Catalina's four new models you select.

If it's the convertible like the one you see here, there's more good news. The top has a brand-new "inward-folding" mechanism that does away with the need for storage compartments at the ends of the seat. About eight more inches of rear seat are now available.

No matter which Catalina you select, however, there's no getting away from such typically value-added features as the fully padded and well-instrumented dash with wood grain framing, thick-padded loop-pile carpet throughout, dual-speed, parallel-action windshield wipers, a new sound-deadening network you wouldn't believe and —oh, yes!—

In 1971 the convertible version of Pontiac's Catalina was in its penultimate year. Convertibles weren't selling well, so the division dropped the drop top from the Catalina line after the 1972 model year.

Pontiac is most famous for models like the GTO of the '60s, the Firebird of the '70s—and even the Fiero of the 1980s. These cars cemented Pontiac's status as a performance car (and pop culture) icon.

Catalina was, at first, Pontiac's entry-level large car, and it came in the full spectrum of body styles—even a station wagon during the car's early years. Sedans and coupes were also built, but the model most treasured as a relic of Pontiac's former glory is the convertible version—particularly those built from 1961 through the final call 11 years later, in 1972, when the last one was christened.

The Catalina was full-size, but it was also the least expensive and lightest of Pontiac's big cars—which made it very popular among big-car performance enthusiasts. As the Kennedy Era dawned, this tendency became an explicit engineering (and marketing) focus.

Nineteen sixty-one marked the first year for the new-style Pontiacs—featuring the now-legendary split grille that became one of Pontiac's signature styling features right through to the end of the division in 2009. (Technically, the first appearance of the split grille theme occurred in 1959—but Pontiac did not fully commit to the look until the '61 model year, when it became an across-the-board motif.)

Catalinas got the new split grille (along with handsome, recessed grille bars and a pair of side-by-side quad headlights), but one of the car's main selling points was Pontiac's wide-track suspension layout, which pushed out the distance between each set of wheels, in order to enhance stability and roadholding. Under the hood, a 389 Trophy V-8 (with either single two- or four-barrel or Tri-Power triple-two-barrel carburetors) could be specified. For the racing circuit, Pontiac even built a handful of Catalinas without the usual warranty—but with a lightened frame and super-thin aluminum bumpers (resulting in about 200 pounds less curb weight) and powered by a radically cammed Super Duty 421 V-8 with twin 500 cfm Carter four barrels and rated at an astounding 405 horsepower.

The true output of the SD-421 was rumored to be in the neighborhood of 460 horsepower. These cars were capable of 12-second (and quicker) quarter-mile times—the equivalent of a 300-pound linebacker who can run a 50-meter sprint in under 6 seconds.

In 1963, the Catalina got a freshened front-end treatment with handsome, vertically stacked headlights and a more squared-off profile. It continued the tradition of full-size performance as the muscle car era officially dawned that fall with the introduction of the intermediate-size, Tempest-based GTO. To distinguish the Catalina from the Goat Pontiac up-sized the Catalina for 1965—increasing its wheelbase to 121 inches (from 120 previously) and restyling the whole works.

The newly stretched '65 Catalina managed the tough trick of being both immensely large yet strikingly sexy. Think Anna Nicole Smith in her best days. Coke-bottle styling similar to the profile used on the smaller GTO—but in the two-liter size—laid the basic template. A proud beak capped the nose, to either side of which sat a pair of vertically stacked headlights with surrounds that canted forward, giving the car a hungry expression.

And it was a hungry thing, no doubt.

For under the hood of every Catalina—even the base model—lay 389 cubic inches of pure Pontiac power, the weakest version of which still produced 256 horsepower sucking through a Rochester two-barrel carburetor. Buyers in search of ramming speed could opt for the four-barrel, higher-compression version of the same basic engine but with 325 horsepower. And if that was insufficient, three two-barrel carbs could be stacked on top (just like in the GTO), bumping things up to 338 horsepower.

Four-speed manual transmissions were available to back these potent Ponchos, too—as well as GM's new Turbo-Hydramatic 400 three-speed automatic transmission—a new design featuring a turbine torque converter that soon became the industry standard.

Period advertising exaggerated the proportions of Pontiac's Catalina convertible to drive home the "wide-track" chassis, as touted by the division's marketing folks.

Catalina: Things to Know

Early Catalinas could be equipped with a portable, battery-powered Sportable Transistor radio that could be taken out of the car.

Pontiac's eight-lug wheels were an unusual design that incorporated the brake drum into the wheels for improved stopping performance. These were a popular option on Catalinas.

During the mid- to late 1960s, Catalina was America's number three best-selling large car, just behind the Ford Galaxie 500 and Chevy Impala.

A short-lived power ventilation system that appeared in 1971 was supposed to provide fresh air to the car's occupants even when the car was stuck in traffic—but became the object of consumer complaints about cold air that could not be turned off.

In 1972, the final year of production, a Catalina convertible carried a base MSRP of $4,080.

A Bonneville was slightly bigger—but not by much (a mere three inches, wheelbase-wise). The Catalina convertible had six inches on the GTO—and spotted it nearly 500 pounds. A V-8 (and a big V-8) was thus mandatory—and would remain so throughout the Catalina's life cycle.

Indeed, Pontiac even offered the formidable 421 HO (a streetable version of this engine with a hydraulic camshaft but still offering up as much as 376 horsepower) as the Catalina's top-of-the-line engine—the core of the 2+2 performance package that first appeared during 1964 and formally transformed the big Pontiac into a kind of oversized GTO.

The 421 HO was not available in the smaller GTO—at least, not as a factory-installed option. If you wanted to play with the big boys, you needed to get yourself a big toy. In addition to the 421 V-8, the 2+2 package also got you a heavy-duty suspension, Hurst-shifted three-speed manual transmission (a four-speed manual was optional), performance axle ratio, and dual exhaust.

Though all Pontiac V-8s are essentially similar (there are no big and small blocks), the 421 was a long-stroke version of the Pontiac V-8 that used a different crankshaft with longer connecting rods to achieve its greater displacement. It was built for high-torque production, as well as high horsepower—the former being as crucial to the acceleration of a two-ton colossus like the Catalina as the latter was to the performance of the comparative lightweight Goat.

So long, that is, as you kept the thing pointed in a straight line.

The 2+2 option did not last long, unfortunately.

It was discontinued after the '67 model year as performance-minded buyers flocked to smaller, more manageable (and better handling) stuff like the GTO and, of course, the new Firebird—which made its debut that year.

Nonetheless, the 2+2's three-year run was enough to establish the Catalina's bona fides as one of the largest true high-performance vehicles ever to be mass produced. More than 40 years later, the survivors are held in high esteem by collectors—especially models with the optional eight-lug rims and manual transmissions. Finding a stick shift in something this massive is a lot like discovering a $50 bill at the bottom of a box of Cracker Jack. It probably shouldn't be there—but you're sure glad it is.

In 1969, Pontiac completely restyled the Catalina—incorporating some of the same motifs used on the same-year Firebird and Tempest/GTO—including an ironing board hood and prominent beak set in the middle of the trademark Pontiac split grille. The four headlights now sat side-by-side instead of vertically stacked. It was not unattractive, but definitely less distinctive, than the 1965–1968s.

On the other hand, it was still a heavyweight mauler.

Wheelbase was up to 122 inches (now 10 full inches longer than the same-year GTO's), and unladen curb weight rose to just 5 pounds under 4,000 pounds.

Another restyle for 1971 brought the B body Catalina's overall dimensions to their high water mark—124 inches of wheelbase and an honest-to-Elvis two-tons-plus (4,081 pounds). Major styling details included a new, Grand Prix–like front-end treatment

CATALINA CONVERTIBLE COUPE

with a heavy-looking vertical grille set behind an equally massive-looking full-length bumper with cow pusher bars on either side of the grille.

Echoes of the ironing board hood remained, but the stamping was more muted. Front buckets with center console and a wide bench in back provide room for five. It was still a very handsome car, top up or down.

The new 400 V-8 (successor to the 389) that first appeared in 1967 was the standard powerplant, rated at 265 horsepower with two-barrel carb. Two 455s (increased bore versions of the old 421/428) were also available, including the 325-horsepower 455 HO—more or less the same engine used in the Trans Am that year but downrated by 10 horsepower. However, the object was not high performance. These huge engines were there for the same reason the Budweiser wagon is pulled along by a team of six Clydesdales. Anything less than 400 cubes would have turned the Catalina into the castrato. The 455 made it all feasible.

With the demise of the 2+2 option after 1967, the Catalina and Bonneville had inadvertently become much closer competitors for the same basic slice of the market—essentially, buyers in search of a boozy, plus-sized cruiser. On this score, the Catalina was at something of a disadvantage since the Bonnie was slightly bigger (125-inch wheelbase in 1969) and thus offered more car (literally) for not much more money.

A '69 Bonneville convertible carried an MSRP of $3,896 versus $3,476 for the equivalent Catalina ragtop.

This closing of the gap may be responsible for the rather sudden death of the Catalina convertible after the '72 run.

The final year of Catalina convertible production saw a slight uptick in sales—about 2,399 were made versus just 2,036 in 1971—as buyers scrambled to get their hands on a piece of big-bodied bodaciousness that was shortly to disappear forever.

The Grand Prix was the convertible for would-be Eurotrash. The Bonneville was the convertible for the most well-heeled of Pontiac's customers. The Catalina was the convertible for the working stiff.

KISSING COUSIN
PONTIAC GRANDVILLE CONVERTIBLE 1971-1975

GRAND VILLE HARDTOP COUPE

GRAND VILLE CONVERTIBLE

Just as Pontiac prepared to excise the Catalina convertible from its lineup, it introduced a new capital ship convertible in its inventory—the mighty (but short-lived) GrandVille.

It was basically a two-door version of the GrandVille sedan, which was now Pontiac's top-of-the-line full-size car, taking over for Bonneville. It had the same wheelbase (126 inches) and overall dimensions as the also full-size Bonneville—but higher status.

Also, the Bonneville was (after 1970) no longer offered in convertible form.

The two-door layout made the GrandVille appear even more massive than a Bonneville sedan because the back two-thirds of the car seemed to go on just about forever. Stand by the driver's side door handle and you were only amidships. If you were a gentleman and wanted to walk around the rear to open the passenger's side door for your companion, she might be waiting a while.

It helped to bring a snack.

Still, the GrandVille carried its weight well. Only the federally mandated five-mile-per-hour bumpers that afflicted the industry across the board in the early to mid-1970s marred the car's otherwise acceptable proportions. They seemed tacked on, an after-thought—which of course, they were. The federales simply dictated that all new cars be so equipped, and rather than restyle entire front and rear clips (which could not be done overnight), Pontiac, like everyone else, drilled a few holes and bolted these equivalents of automotive orthodontia onto the poor GrandVille (and every other model, too).

Thus, it is the earlier models, from 1971–1972, that are the most cosmetically appealing—with their baleen whale–like screen of a grille unobstructed by the chromed 2x4 grafted onto the '73 and later versions. A bumper was there, but it was more like a chrome-plated chin that sat underneath the grillework.

Four hundred and fifty-five cubic inches of power was absolutely standard in the 4,266-pound GrandVille—and it was absolutely necessary. In 1971, the year GM began throttling high-compression engines, a first step in the long slide into the emissions-emasculated mid-1970s, Chief Many Horses ponied up 325 of them—virtually the same output of the same-year Trans Am in 455 HO form but in a more stately package. Argent or body-colored 15x7 rally wheels and rear fender skirts (from 1973 up) completed the ensemble.

Grand Ville Convertible in Porcelain Blue.

GrandVille: Things to Know

Though most GrandVilles were heavily optioned with luxury equipment, it was possible to order one without AC, power windows—or even a passenger-side door mirror.

No GrandVille ever weighed less than 4,000 pounds—or ever had anything smaller than a 455-cubic-inch V-8 under its 150-pound stamped-steel hood.

All GrandVilles had four headlights—the better to see you with, my pretty!

Champagne, Spring Blue, and Glacier White were popular '70s colors. A very rare option for 1974 was adjustable pedals.

GrandVille was one of Pontiac's shortest-lived models, lasting just five years in production before being cancelled. Total convertible production over the period 1971–1975 was 15,968—with the lowest production year being the first year, 1971, when about 1,789 were built.

In 1972, the lower bumper began its inexorable rise upward, now splitting the already split grille horizontally as well as vertically. The GV's standard 455 suffered a myocardial infarct at this time, too—leaving it crippled down to 185 horsepower. Even though the way horsepower ratings were published had been changed from way-optimistic SAE "gross" to a more honest SAE "net" (engine installed in the car, with accessories and with a factory stock tune), this was a calamitous decline.

Fortunately, the GV's honor could still be preserved by ordering the optional 220-horsepower version of the gradually fading away 455.

Models from 1973 got the ugly bumpers (with cow pusher bars on both ends) and a less angry-looking grille treatment. The headlight buckets now drooped down into the grille, making the big Pontiac seem sad.

On the upside, the standard 455 was kick-started a bit, up to 215 horsepower—and you could order a 250-horsepower version with dual exhaust and Quadrajet four barrel. GTO-like three-bar taillights still looked sharp from the rear, too. These would be altered to full-length, blocked style for 1974—a look that wasn't nearly as clean or attractive as previously but that made Uncle Sam happy because the brake lights were more visible now. Pontiac tried to revisit the grille shape of the 1971–1972s, but the presence of that girder-like, rub-strip-coated battering ram of a bumper could not disappear by cosmetic trickery.

This (1974) would also be the last year before catastrophic converters put a choke hold on the 455. Up to 255 horsepower was still there for the taking, power put to the ground through a beefy THM400 three-speed automatic. The engine even had dual exhausts.

The year 1975 brought the dreaded cats, single exhaust only, and no more than 200 horsepower, SAE net. And that was with the optional engine. The base 455 was back to a droopy 185. A new front clip with four rectangular headlights also appeared—and "Brougham" was added to the nomenclature. But only briefly. Pontiac dropped the GrandVille—part and parcel of GM's across-the-board cancellation of convertibles. About 4,519 of them were made during the Final Call.

Beginning with the '76 model year, Bonneville once again became Pontiac's top-of-the-line (and largest) model. However, it was smaller than the last of the GrandVilles (riding on a trimmed-down 124-inch wheelbase), and forget about a ragtop version; these would not make a comeback for nearly a decade (until the mid-1980). Big Poncho convertibles never would.

The '75 B-body GrandVille was truly the last of the Mohicans. It now dwells with the Great Spirit—along with Pontiac itself.

YOU WANT A MAN'S CAR
CHRYSLER 300 CONVERTIBLE
1969-1970

The largest, most powerful battleship ever made was the World War II–era Japanese Yamato and her sister ship, Musashi. They came late to the war and didn't survive it—in part because they were just too massive to hide themselves from the swarms of Allied dive bombers that eventually sent them to the bottom.

A parallel fate befell the Chrysler 300 convertible.

Descended from the famous letter series high-performance (and high luxury) line of large Chryslers that dated back to 1955, the 300 convertible had been designated with letters following the 300 up until the 1965 300 M. After that the final letter was dropped, and the car became simply the 300. Chrysler was apparently trying to shift its marketing strategy for these cars by fiddling with the nomenclature. It was believed that the letter series designations had become a liability, as sales of these lead-bellied large Chryslers had been flagging for several years.

However, the truth is this was more likely due not to any defect with the names but simply because of the demographic shift of the early to mid-1960s. The new crop of baby boomers liked their performance cars closer to Mustang-size, and meanwhile the older cadres who favored the fulsome were getting beyond their tire-frying years. They were gravitating toward more sedately configured steamships and had no use for the big guns of the Yamato-like letter cars.

In 1969 Chrysler's 300 featured what corporate marketing literature referred to as "fuselage styling." No one was quite sure what that meant.

27

When Chrysler introduced the 300 series in 1955, it was the most powerful car you could buy, a true muscle car for well-heeled enthusiasts. By 1970, the final year of production for the convertible 300, the big car still had plenty of muscle from its 375-horse, 440-cubic-inch V-8.

While the 300 series had plenty of muscle and really didn't weigh that much more than the muscle cars from Dodge and Plymouth, the cushy, well-appointed interior set the car apart from its Spartan muscle-car cousins.

Still, there would be one last run for glory—just like the one-way trip of the famous Japanese battlewagon in the autumn of 1945.

It would begin in 1969.

Riding on Chrysler's largest wheelbase (124 inches), a 300 convertible easing into the road called forth images of an F-8 Crusader turning into the wind, afterburner lit, and flaps down.

The ordnance it carried was just as impressive. No less than a big-block 440 four-barrel powered the 300. It made 350 horsepower and 480 lbs-ft of torque. And it was merely the standard engine. Buyers could arm up even more heavily by selecting the optional TNT version of the 440—and enjoy the bullying force of its 375 horsepower. A three-speed Torqueflite automatic came with either engine.

One of the many things that makes these 300 convertibles so special today was their very low production back in the day. In 1969, only 1,933 were built—versus 16,075 hardtop coupes and another 14,464 sedans. The totals in 1970 were even slimmer—just 1,077 were made. With a combined two-year production of barely more than 3,000 cars, Chrysler decided to drop the 300 convertible.

It would be the last five-passenger ragtop built by Chrysler, but at least it went out with a bang—just like the Yamato some 25 years previously.

300: Things to Know

In 1971, Chrysler offered a Hurst conversion package that, according to official records, was available only with hardtop coupe versions of the 300. However, some claim that at least a handful of Hurst 300 convertibles were made. If true, they would be among the rarest and most collectible of Mopars.

Base price for the '69 300 convertible was $5,060 versus $4,714 for the hardtop coupe. In 1970, the base price rose to $5,195 (convertibles), while hardtop coupes listed for $4,849.

The 300 hardtop coupe lasted until the end of the '71 model year, after which it was dropped. Production by then had declined to just 7,256 examples.

In 1979, Chrysler resurrected the 300 nameplate and used it for a specially modified, high-performance version of the Cordoba coupe. It came with a 195-horsepower 360 V-8 but was never available in convertible form.

The full-size Newport convertible shared the 300's 124-inch wheelbase (also the same as the New Yorker sedan's) and general outsized dimensions but not its performance emphasis. However, like the 300 convertible, the '70 Newport convertible was made in exceedingly small numbers. Just 1,124 for 1970.

FANTASTIC FORD
GALAXIE 500/XL/LTD CONVERTIBLE 1968-1972

2-Door Hardtop and Convertible... Car buffs can tell right off, these are *performance* cars... styled and equipped for just one thing—action! The 7-Litre Hardtop and Convertible are an all-new order for those who demand real "go" in the cars they drive.

"7-Litre" badges on grille and fenders hint strongly at what's under the hood—the mighty, new Thunderbird 428 V-8. It's 345 hp strong, with 4-barrel carburetor, hydraulic lifters and special dual, low-restriction exhaust. Standard too are Cruise-O-Matic Drive (with T-bar console-mounted shift lever), power front disc brakes, styled steel wheel covers and distinctive 7-Litre body striping. (Other 7-Litre standard equipment same as listed for XL's on pages 8 and 9.)

Now move inside one of these spirited new Fords. Deep-foam shell buckets up front (as shown on page 9). Genuine walnut in between. Leather-smooth vinyl trim (choice of seven colors) all around. Seat belts fore and aft. Padded instrument panel and sun visors. Glass rear window in the convertible ... and that's just the beginning. With 7-Litre options, you can go all out for performance, or balance performance with luxury. Cobra 427 V-8 with 425 hp, 4-speed stick shift, limited-slip differential, heavy-duty suspension ... new Stereo, power steering, power windows and power seats.

For all its pure driving fun 7-Litres offer, they also offer great practicalities like the suspended accelerator pedal, reversible keys and Ford's Twice-a-Year Maintenance ... features that make owning *any* new Ford more fun.

Galaxie 500 7-Litre Convertible; also available in XL Series

Ford cancelled its big convertibles several years before either GM or Chrysler bowed before the new reality that government—as much as consumers—would dictate what kinds of new cars would be built.

The popular story is that rising gas prices killed off big cars—and with them, big convertibles. But the truth is that gas prices (and shortages) were just one of the factors that drove big cars off the cliff—at least, as mass-production vehicles available to people of average means.

The other big factor was Washington's increasing micromanagement of the car industry and, specifically, proposed roof crush standards that automakers feared would be imposed as summarily (and without regard to cost) as were the first slew of emissions control mandates that came down on their collective noggins like an anvil dropped from the top of a 10-story building. Ford especially did not want to find itself in the position of having to slap-dashedly redesign its ragtops to appease the safety brownshirts. Better to just drop 'em before it became impossible to build 'em.

But Ford would let loose a final Rebel Yell of defiance—in the form of the biggest, meanest, most fearsome convertibles to ever carry the Blue Oval crest.

Originally, the Galaxie was simply a Fairlane with upgraded trim. As such, it was Ford's top-of-the-line convertible when the nameplate was introduced mid-year 1969. Eventually it ceded the top spot in the lineup to the Galaxie XL and then to the LTD.

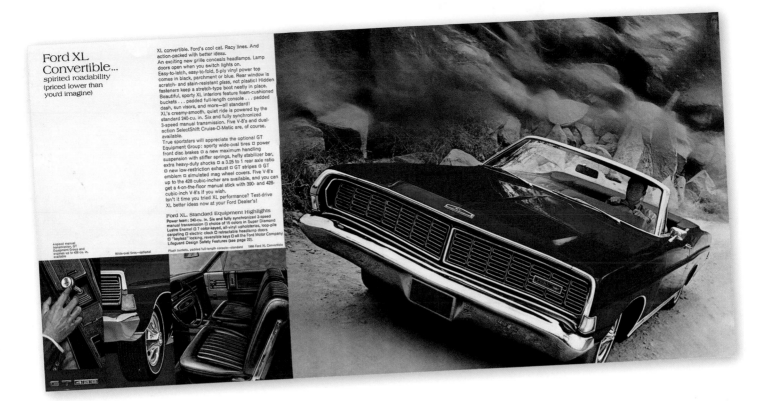

Ford XL
Convertible...
spirited roadability
(priced lower than
you'd imagine)

XL convertible. Ford's cool cat. Racy lines. And action-packed with better ideas. An exciting new grille conceals headlamps. Lamp doors open when you switch lights on. Easy-to-latch, easy-to-fold, 5-ply vinyl power top comes in black, parchment or blue. Rear window is scratch- and stain-resistant glass, not plastic! Hidden fasteners keep a stretch-type boot neatly in place. Beautiful, sporty XL interiors feature foam-cushioned buckets . . . padded full-length console . . . padded dash, sun visors, and more—all standard! XL's creamy-smooth, quiet ride is powered by the standard 240-cu. in. Six and fully synchronized 3-speed manual transmission. Five V-8's and dual-action SelectShift Cruise-O-Matic are, of course, available. True sportsters will appreciate the optional GT Equipment Group: sporty wide-oval tires ◻ power front disc brakes ◻ a new maximum handling suspension with stiffer springs, hefty stabilizer bar, extra heavy-duty shocks ◻ a 3.25 to 1 rear axle ratio ◻ new low-restriction exhaust ◻ GT stripes ◻ GT emblem ◻ simulated mag wheel covers. Five V-8's up to the 428 cubic-incher are available, and you can get a 4-on-the-floor manual stick with 390- and 428-cubic-inch V-8's if you wish. Isn't it time you tried XL performance? Test-drive XL better ideas now at your Ford Dealer's!

Ford XL. Standard Equipment Highlights
Power team: 240-cu. in. Six and fully synchronized 3-speed manual transmission ◻ choice of 15 colors in Super Diamond Lustre Enamel ◻ 7 color-keyed, all-vinyl upholsteries, loop-pile carpeting ◻ electric clock ◻ retractable headlamp doors ◻ "keyless" locking, reversible keys ◻ all the Ford Motor Company Lifeguard Design Safety Features (see page 22).

4-speed manual transmission, GT Equipment Group and engines up to 428 cu. in. available

Wide-oval tires—optional

Plush buckets, padded full-length console—standard   1968 Ford XL Convertible

GT 428

For 1968, Ford didn't alter the bodywork much on its full-sized cars, but the switch from vertically stacked headlights to quad headlights laid out horizontally made a dramatic change in the appearance of the cars.

Galaxie 500/XL/LTD Convertible: Things to Know

The year 1959 was the first for Galaxie 500 convertibles; base price for a Sunliner was $2,839. Curb weight was 3,578 pounds.

The '68 Galaxie 500 was available in 15 different colors and offered no less than 30 different upholstery choices.

While earlier-year Galaxie 500s could be ordered with manual transmissions, by 1971 the standard (only) transmission offered was Ford's three-speed Cruise-O-Matic automatic.

The big 429 V-8 that first appeared in 1969 got even bigger after 1972, when an overbore bulked it up to 460 cubic inches. Only Cadillac's 500-cubic-inch V-8 was bigger.

The year 1972 was the last for a full-size Ford convertible, with a base price of $4,057 and a curb weight of 4,165 pounds.

It's hard to pin down exactly when the Galaxie 500 convertible ceased to exist—in name as well as fact.

Some say 1970, the year when, at least officially—the Galaxie 500 came only in hardtop coupe, sedan, and station wagon varieties. But you could still get virtually the same car, as a convertible, under the XL nameplate. Then in 1971, ragtops were technically LTDs (and again in 1972).

All, however, rode on the same 121-inch wheelbase (after 1969), shared the same chassis (what moderns call a platform), and were among the final run of truly fulsome Fords—two-door convertibles that stretched a foot or more beyond the outer limits of modern "full-size" four-door sedans, drank gas with greater gusto than a Hummer, and could get the better of one in a fender-bender, too.

Cars were more manly and menacing in those days—before anyone except a few quavering geeks cared much about safety. What mattered was how big your V-8 was. And the Galaxie 500/XL/LTD carried a very big V-8, indeed—seven liters' worth of 428 four-barrel, making 340 horsepower (in 1968) and also making the life of your back tires short—and your trips to the Sunoco station frequent.

Despite their size and the ferocity of which these things were capable, they were also stately—built more for leisurely top-down sauntering. A prime example of this was the opening sequence of the Charleton Heston classic, *The Omega Man*, in which we see our hero blasting robed, light-hating mutants with a machine gun from behind the wheel of a red convertible LTD.

Plenty of room for target acquisition—and just the ticket for running down the strays.

One of the car's signature features is something rarely seen today—vacuum-actuated headlight doors

that kept the front end looking seamless during daytime operation. These got dropped later on, though—mostly on account of problems with the doors not opening when they should, not opening all the way—or failing to close completely.

As these cars got bigger (wheelbase and weight reached high tide by 1972) so did the roster of available creature features. Everything from a six-way power driver's seat to SelectAire air conditioning was on the menu. Popular options included power windows and door locks, tilt wheel, and AM/FM stereo with two (count 'em!) speakers on the rear package shelf. A Brougham trim/equipment upgrade bought you most of these big-ticket options in a single package.

Convertibles—Galaxie 500, XL, LTD, and otherwise—went away for good after 1972, though the Galaxie nameplate lasted another few innings, until 1975. That year, the LTD took over as the biggest Ford you could still buy. Amazingly, Ford continued to build these 121-inch-wheelbased whales all the way through to 1979—two or three years after both GM and Ford had thrown in the towel and begun frantically downsizing their cars across the board. Ford even hinted at a possible resurgence of the convertible with the introduction of the Landau (in 1975), which carried a faint whiff of open-aired possibility, just maybe.

But by 1979 the party was over for good with the introduction of the short-wheelbase LTD II. Convertibles by this time were not just a fond memory; they had become an impossibility. At least, in full-size form. Ford would eventually offer cars with ragtops, but they would all be micro-sized tugboats compared with the audacious dreadnoughts of the late 1960s and early 1970s.

We who were there were privileged to know them . . .

And we shall not forget!

Upgrading from a pedestrian Galaxie to an XL or LTD got you a number of added features, the most obvious of which were hidden headlights.

CHAPTER 2

LOW-RENT LIMOS

Near Luxury for Those with Cadillac Tastes
But Oldsmobile Budgets

Ford LTD
AMC Ambassador
Buick Electra 225
Chevy Impala
Chevy Caprice
Oldsmobile 98 Regency

FULSOME FORD LTD
1965-1982

IF YOU'VE NEVER OWNED A FORD,
YOU'RE ONE OF THE REASONS WE BUILT THIS LTD.

LTD Country Squire features richly sculptured woodlike paneling . . . new die-cast grille with retractable headlamp doors

LTD standard interior, handsomely tailored, has plush fabrics softer, silkier, more lustrous than before

New luxury-size LTD for 1969 is unlike any car in its class. Many compare it with America's most expensive cars. And that's quite easy to understand.

The LTD hugs the road with as wide a track as a Cadillac. It smooths your ride with a 121-in. wheelbase. And it is designed to ride even quieter than the LTD that was quieter than a Rolls-Royce.

LTD also offers surprising maneuverability and easy handling. It U-turns in an even smaller radius than last year's Ford of exceptional roadability.

LTD's quiet ride comes from refinements beyond extra soundproofing. It's built in with a rugged new "S" frame, new body mounts that adapt to varying road conditions and improvements that isolate vibration so well— you ride in recording-studio-quiet.

LTD Country Squire

You enjoy the same serene elegance in the impressive new '69 LTD Country Squire. Wagonmaster innovations emphasize Ford wagon leadership everywhere. A new 3-way Magic Doorgate opens as a door . . . glass up or down . . . for passengers, and flips down as a tailgate for cargo.

Foam-cushioned seats, upholstered in beautifully pleated glove-soft vinyl ! . . . woodlike touches, plus other lavish appointments, give you luxury, comfort and convenience on a grand scale uncommon in the popular-price class.

Your Ford Dealer invites you to discover LTD luxury with a test drive.

LTD 4-Door Sedan with vinyl roof option

Ford completely redesigned its full-size sedans for the 1969 model year, stretching the wheelbase from 119 inches to 121 inches.

Previous pages: **The convertible version** of the Caprice Classic soldiered on through the 1975 model year.

Ford is now the last U.S. automaker standing on its own two feet; Ford came through the Great Tumult of 2009 as the only American car company not strapped to an IV infusion of government dole.

It also built what will likely prove the final source waters of a nearly extinct species of automobilus Americanus familiaris—the mass-produced low-rent limo. A garage stuffer every inch as long (and every pound as heavy) as $50,000 BMW and Benz sedans but for half the money and without the fun-snuffing overactive electronic mommas that won't let you stand on the brakes and floor the gas until the V-8 up front melts the rear tires down to the cords.

The last of these, the Crown Victoria and its higher-trimmed Mercury sister—the Grand Marquis—are the glowing embers of what was once a mighty bonfire. They are

living reminders of a time when such cars were the rule rather than the exception—a time when the 1970s-era incarnation of Joe the Plumber had access to wide-bodied wonders, too.

One of the Late Greats was named LTD.

No one knows for sure just exactly what LTD stands for. Some say "Limited"—others "Luxury Trim Decor." Perhaps there is an ancient temple somewhere with weathered letters chiseled in stone, signifying "Don't let the door slam closed on your finger"—or "room for six, budget rates."

Regardless of the precise meaning, we know the LTD crest has been used as submodel script on a variety of Ford's vehicles over the years—including the '70s-era Torino and the '80s-era Taurus. But the car with which it is most properly affiliated was the automaker's near-luxury large sedans that roamed the roads from 1965 through 1982.

LTD began life as a high-trimmed Galaxie 500—riding on the same 119-inch wheelbase and displacing 3,578 pounds. It was about four inches longer, wheelbase-wise, than a same-year Fairlane 500—and about 600 pounds heavier. Base price was $3,313 and Ford sold close to 70,000 of them that first year out.

The concept behind the LTD was to outdo the Chevy (Caprice) as well as Dodge (Polara) and others who had glommed on to the idea of selling what amounted to a working man's Caddy—a big car with lots of upmarket amenities and a family-guy price tag.

Ford, once the number one brand in America, had long since relinquished its crown to Chevrolet by 1965, but the company still attempted to compete with its larger rival at every opportunity. When Chevrolet introduced the upscale Caprice, Ford responded by introducing the LTD, a more luxurious version of its Galaxie sedan.

In addition to hidden headlights, Ford stylists gave the 1968 LTD a more formal roofline to distinguish it from the proletariat Galaxie models.

**LTD Brougham.
Inside quiet
...infinite comfort.**

An infinitely luxurious Brougham interior surrounds you with better ideas in comfort. Like roominess to relax and stretch out, thanks to the spacious Ford Front Room with unique swept-away instrument panel.

Gauges and controls are easy to see, easy to reach. They're clustered in a curved cockpit arrangement before the driver. An electric clock and woodtone appliques are included. Nice touches, we think.

And there are helpful lights where you want them, in the glove compartment. Luggage compartment. As front and rear doors open. Even in the ash tray.

In front, the deep-cushioned High Back bench seat has a wide, plush center armrest. The optional split bench version, individually adjustable, gives you a dual center armrest and the reclining passenger seat. A blessing on long trips. Available are 6-Way Power Seats—driver only or full-width—for more convenience.

Besides the look of luxury, there's a new touch and feel of luxury. Lustrous new cloth and vinyl fabrics, soft and supple, come in black, dark red, medium blue, medium green, gray gold or tobacco. Thick cut-pile carpeting, in the same decorator colors, adds elegance to the floor.

There are peace of mind comforts, too. Sturdy, side-door Guard Rails designed for greater passenger security. Uni-Lock Harness to keep you snug. And a host of other standard Ford Motor Company Lifeguard Design Safety Features. See the list on page 20.

You can add more luxuries on your own, of course. SelectAire Conditioner with Automatic Temperature Control. Power door locks. Power side windows. AM/FM Stereo Radio that makes you think the musicians are in the car. Stereosonic Tape System, which makes you your own entertainment director. You'll find other better idea options on pages 18 and 19.

Take a comfortable Quiet Break soon in the LTD Brougham.

Spacious LTD Brougham, High Back bench seat with luxurious, Dark Red nylon cloth and vinyl fabric

Brougham originally referred to a small, four-wheeled, horse-drawn carriage with an enclosed passenger compartment. By the 1970s, American auto manufacturers began applying the word to cars, apparently denoting interiors that would make a prostitute blush.

Buyers could get their hands on power windows and door locks, air conditioning, eight-track stereos, and a better cut of interior trim than was common on most of the Blue Light Specials of the era.

The presence of at least eight cylinders under the hood (versus the depressing inline sixes used as base engines on the bottom feeders) was another clear point of departure.

In its inaugural year, the LTD came standard with Ford's highly respected 289-cubic-inch small-block V-8, in either two-barrel Lo Po (200 horsepower) or four-barrel Hi-Po (271 horsepower) forms, the latter of which was essentially the same K engine used that year in the Mustang GT.

Larger V-8s, including the powerhouse 390 and 427 big-blocks, could be ordered optionally.

Success was immediate, and based on this, Ford spun off the LTD as a separate model in its own right for 1967. It still shared a platform (chassis/frame and basic nuts and bolts) with the Galaxie 500 but had put some real distance between itself and that budget-minded big 'un. The Galaxie notched down a peg and became Ford's volume model (130,063 sedans were sold during 1967) while the LTD became Ford's fanciest roller. Its base price of $3,298—which was about $600 higher than a base Galaxie sedan—reflected this.

The '67 LTD was a sharp-looking car, its front end defined by a pair of vertically stacked and forward-canted headlights set between a bar-type grille. There was a hint of T-Bird in the formal roofline—which naturally could be further pompadoured with vinyl topcoat. Sporty aluminum trim along the lower rocker panels and turbine-style wheel covers added flair. The trunk, meanwhile, was hot tub huge. With a few tubes of RTV to make it watertight, you could fill it up and either take a dip or provide a home on-the-go for several sea bass.

Inside were low-back, three-across bench seats; a 120-mile-per-hour speedo (with redline beginning at 70, the then typical highway speed limit); and a fuel gauge off to the left. These two instruments told you the two most important things to know about your new LTD: How fast? And: How much gas is left?

Underneath the speedo was a secondary array of indicators for oil pressure, temperature, and alternator (later models got idiot lights).

The passenger-side glove box area could be finished with handsome fake wood trim, and the door panels boasted their own armrest—with individual ashtrays all around. Shoulder belts, however, were nowhere to be found. The safety Nazis had not yet prevailed—and LTD drivers were still free to drive without being strapped in like Apollo astronauts for each trip to the corner gas 'n' go.

Color choices included classics such as Light Tobacco Bronze—a choice of words that would surely arouse a frenzy of concerned-mom letter writing in these politically correct times.

In 1969, a major makeover added hidden headlights—as well as a few more pounds. Actually more like 400 pounds. An LTD sedan now bellied up to the bar at nearly 3,900 pounds. Wheelbase was extended to 121 inches, too—making the '69 the longest and heaviest LTD to date. The quad headlights were now horizontally arranged, and there was the hint of a beak in the tapered tip of the nosecone.

Like an aging jock with man breasts where pecs once were, pendulous bumpers hung off the revised front end, which lost its headlight doors after 1970 (these would make a comeback, like Elvis, in subsequent years). But the LTD still could be had with the colossal 429 V-8 under its hood, if the prospective buyer checked off that option.

Otherwise, a 302-cubic-inch small-block was standard.

The LTD, like virtually every other full-framed, cholesterol-choked Americano road hog, was paddling choppy waters as the '70s progressed. Ford saw that the future did not look bright ahead but nonetheless put on a brave face, crossed its fingers, and redid the car for 1973—without liposuctioning the life out of the thing. If anything, the '73 had bulked up; it now weighed in at well over 4,000 pounds, a true titan fully worthy of Oscar Goldman or Steve McGarrett. (LTDs were a common sight in '70s-era TV shows such as *Hawaii Five-O* and *CHiPs*.)

The look was more stolid—the veritable breadbox on wheels—which Ford can't be blamed for as much as the government. Suffocating bumper-impact standards made it next to impossible to deviate from a basic shape that was more or less bricklike.

Still, it was an impressive sight. In silver or light blue, all that seemed missing was the conning tower and a battery of 16-inch guns. There would have been ample room on the fantail to paint a helicopter landing pad—and with a few missile launch tubes along the flanks, an LTD would have been a fair facsimile of the USS Iowa during its first Gulf War sortie.

Ford may have been a step and a half down the ladder from Lincoln, but the interior of the LTD was still a pretty inviting place.

LTD LANDAU

A new, luxurious standard-size car designed to replace longer, heavier, more expensive cars.

Ford presents the distinctive new LTD Landau. Easily one of the most luxurious Fords ever built. With fine-car features, plus prestigious styling certain to challenge that of more expensive cars.

Both the 2-Door and 4-Door Pillared Hardtops are proud ways to get a lot of car for your money. Each gives you nearly all the things you'd want from a costlier car. And LTD Landau does it without adding a lot of unnecessary weight and size.

In cost of ownership, you'll find that the new LTD Landau gives you a lot of standard equipment for what you pay—including gas-saving radial ply tires. You get a maintenance schedule that helps make LTD Landau economical to own. It is so distinctively styled and well-made it is designed to maintain popularity and hold its value until you're ready to trade again.

LTD Landau offers outstanding features, standard. Hidden headlamps, for distinctive styling. Vinyl roof. Wide new color-keyed vinyl bodyside moldings. Front cornering lamps that help you see into turns. Wheel covers. And that's just outside.

Equally impressive are interior luxuries. Flight bench seat, with a fold-down armrest, trimmed with lush Knit Cloth. Padded door panels. Cut-pile carpeting. Right- and left-hand remote control mirrors. Automatic parking brake release. Electric trunk lid release.

Going for LTD Landau are great features like a 351 2V V-8 engine. SelectShift transmission. Power steering. Power front disc brakes, and more. Check the Notable Standard Features list below.

When it comes to options, Ford offers a wide variety of ways in which you can design more driving fun. Which is also why we say the Landau is a sensible alternative to longer, heavier, more expensive cars. The closer you look, the better we look.

LTD Landau 4-Door Pillared Hardtop puts fine-car luxury within reach. Silver Blue Glow (Code 3M) with Blue vinyl roof and matching wide vinyl bodyside moldings.

NOTABLE STANDARD FEATURES—LTD Landau
Functional—351-cu. in. 2V V-8 with Solid State Ignition □ SelectShift Cruise-O-Matic Transmission □ Power Front Disc Brakes □ Power Steering □ Steel-Belted Radial Ply Black Sidewall Tires □ Front Bumper Guards □ Front Cornering Lamps □ Wiper-Mounted Washer Jets □ Electric Clock □ Power Ventilation □ Convenience Group □ Lights in Glove and Luggage Compartment, Center Ash Tray □ Front Door Courtesy Lights □ Rear Door Courtesy Light Switches □ Inside Hood Release □ LTD Sound Package □ All Ford Motor Company Lifeguard Design Safety Features like side door beams, protective bumpers, and many others.
Appearance & Comfort—Flight Bench Seat with Center Armrest □ Niles Knit Cloth and Vinyl Trim □ Bright Pedal Trim □ Deluxe Steering Wheel □ Color-Keyed Deluxe Belts □ Bright Seat Side Shields □ Automatic Seat Back Release (2-Door) □ Color-Keyed Cut-Pile Carpeting □ Woodtone Instrument Panel and Door Applique □ Vinyl Roof □ Hood Ornament □ Wide Vinyl Insert Bodyside Moldings □ Bright Windsplit, Fender Peak, Hood Rear, Door Belt, Drip Rail, Taillamp, Quarter and Window Moldings □ Center Pillar Windows (2-Door) □ "C" Pillar Crest (4-Door) □ Wheel Covers.

MEASUREMENTS
Wheelbase 121.0" □ Length 223.9" □ Height 53.7" (2-Dr.), 54.8" (4-Dr.) □ Width 79.5" □ Fuel Capacity and Type (gal.) 24.2, Unleaded □ Curb Weight (lb.) 2-Dr. Pillared Hardtop 4625, 4-Dr. Pillared Hardtop 4657 □ Passenger Capacity—6.

LTD Landau 2-Door Hardtop in Candyapple Red (Code 2E) with Dark Red vinyl roof.

Landau Luxury Group. Easy way to add plush comfort. ▶
Now you can enjoy salon elegance and bask in compliments to your good taste. New Landau Luxury Group option gives you the sumptuous split bench seat with dual front seat armrests as shown, and passenger recliner, for superb lounge chair comfort. You also get:
□ Impeccable tailoring in 100% nylon luxury Knit Cloth with the look and feel of cashmere □ 22-oz. shag carpeting front and rear □ Burled walnut woodtone instrument panel applique (see right) □ Front and rear door pull straps, front seat-back assist straps that let passengers enter and exit gracefully (shown below) □ Digital clock □ Luxury door and quarter trim panels with woven carpeting on lower door panels (except when White vinyl trim is ordered) □ Lights where you want them, including an illuminated visor vanity mirror □ Luxury steering wheel □ Super sound package, and more □ Besides Blue (Code KB) shown, Green, Saddle, Tan and Dark Red are available.

◀ **Standard LTD Landau interior. Luxurious as it comes.**
Impressive standard Landau interior features a soft, yet durable, luxurious Niles Knit Cloth shown in Dark Red (Code HD). Black, Blue, Green, Saddle or Tan are other color choices. All-vinyl trim, in the same colors, except Black, is optional. White all-vinyl can be ordered on 2-Door models. Flight bench seat, with a single plush center armrest, is deep-cushioned for comfort. Note padded door panels with woodtone accents. Convenience Group refinements like right- and left-hand remote control mirrors, automatic parking brake release, electric trunk lid release, and more.

3

Notes: See Notable Standard Features above. Other items shown are optional. See Color Code reference on back cover.

4

Landau is a city in what was once southern Rhineland. What that has to do with luxury automobiles is anyone's guess, but given that the name *Brougham* was becoming something of a cliché by the mid-1970s, manufacturers had to come up with some name for the most tarted-up versions of their cars.

Perhaps the best part about the mid-'70s LTD, though, was the availability of the second-biggest V-8 ever offered in an American car. An astounding 460 cubes were at your disposal. To get bigger—and thirstier—you had to step up to a Cadillac. In the Ford line, even Lincoln offered nothing larger. The 460's single-digit appetite for regular unleaded is also something whose like we shall not see again.

Another interesting thing about the 460 is it holds the distinction of being one of the least powerful huge engines ever made—barely cresting 200 horsepower in its final years of production.

America's bicentennial year was also the last year for a truly large LTD—and also the 460 V-8, which Ford simply could not bring forth any longer without risking a beating from the EPA.

Despite the new reality, a decently redone LTD appeared in 1977, and this car soldiered on through 1982 with its standard V-8, rear-drive layout and boxy-but-accommodating bodywork unmolested.

Legions were pressed into service as taxis and cop cars—where sturdy features, such as a solid rear axle and the availability of both the 302 and 351 V-8s, made it virtually indestructible as well as ideal for bouncing over curbs at 30 miles per hour or idling in front of hotels and airports for hours on end, AC blasting away.

In 1983, the curtain came down for good on the LTD when the almost-compact Fairmont sedan showed up—and the Crown Vic became Ford's last-man-standing large sedan.

Ford continued to mount the LTD crest on various models and continues to do so to this day. But for the most part, these have been thin-blooded pretenders unworthy of the name.

1980 FORD
LTD

Rides as quiet as a
Rolls-Royce.

LTD: Things to Know

The LTD's push-button AM/FM stereo was marketed as "Aeronutronic"—the Ford equivalent of "rich, Corinthian leather."

Ford advertised the '73 LTD as being "quieter at 60 mph than an airborne glider."

A '75 LTD with the 351 V-8 heaved itself to 60 in 13 seconds while slurping gas at the rate of 9.5 miles per gallon, according to the *Road & Track* 1974 new car preview.

In the first *Terminator* movie, Kyle Reese and Sarah Connor try to avoid Arnold in a blue LTD. Another apocalyptic LTD is featured in the 1971 Charleton Heston classic, *The Omega Man*— during which Heston's character machine-guns mutants from the front seat of a red LTD convertible.

The LTD Brougham was as close to a Lincoln Town Car as you could get without actually ponying up for a Lincoln.

Ford came late to the downsizing game. Chevrolet had downsized the Caprice Classic in 1977. Ford didn't get around to producing a more rationally sized LTD until 1979, but when the company finally did, designers shrunk the beast by a full 15 inches. It was still monstrously huge, however.

AMC'S ALMIGHTY
AMBASSADOR
1965-1974

The *Ambassador* nameplate was originally used by Nash, one of the companies that became American Motors Corporation (AMC), after which the Ambassador was transferred to Rambler. Ultimately, the Ambassador became AMC's flagship luxury car.

V·8
AMBASSADOR
6

ONE OF 3 SENSIBLE SPECTACULARS—1965 RAMBLER AMBASSADOR
...largest and finest of the new RAMBLERS

American Motors Corporation was once America's fourth-largest automaker—bigger than Nissan is today—and can be credited with a number of noteworthy innovations, both in terms of its business practices and in terms of the cars the company made.

For example, while AMC was criticized back in the day for its use of parts and components made by other automakers, this practice—which was not widespread in the '50s and '60s—has become absolutely commonplace today. AMC pioneered cost savings by farming out the manufacture of parts that weren't critical to the identity of the vehicle itself, such as power steering pumps and so on.

On the product side, AMC was one of the first U.S. car companies to offer overdrive transmissions (Twin Stick) decades before overdrive transmissions became a common

spectacular luxury–sensible handling ease
Rambler Ambassador 990 4-Door Sedan

Rambler presents spectacular sedan beauty and luxury—200 exquisite inches of it—in a car that remains among America's easiest to park and handle. Much greater trunk room, too. Choose from two smart models—the 990 (illustrated) and the 880. Both offer full six-passenger room for all the family. New Lustre-Gard Acrylic Enamel in 14 colors and 52 optional two-tone combinations give longer paint life.

Real jewel-like elegance is represented in the 1965 Ambassador instrument panel. Gauges and indicators are conveniently grouped in two large instrument dials located for easy driver vision. Electric wipers, optional.

This is but one of the many rich upholstery combinations available in Rambler Ambassador. Spectacular is the word for Ambassador's decorator-styled interiors. The vinyl-covered instrument-panel padding curves gracefully into the doors. Simulated wood-grain door and panel inserts add a smart accent.

feature on American cars. AMC was also the first American car company to include air conditioning as standard equipment in one of its vehicles, the Ambassador.

But it was AMC's self-initiated transformation from a manufacturer of fairly small, efficient cars to purveyor of heavy metal battlewagons that may ultimately have sealed the company's doom.

Beginning in the mid-1960s, AMC decided to try to compete directly with the Big Three with a full lineup of cars, including large (and destined to grow larger) sedans, wagons, and coupes—rather than continue its tradition of economy and efficiency. When the market did a sudden and unexpected U-turn in the early '70s as a result of rising gas prices and gas shortages, AMC found itself stuck in the same sinking boat as its Motor City rivals.

Ironically, had it stayed the course pioneered by Hudson and Nash, AMC probably could have weathered the '70s—and might still be around today.

But then, of course, we would never have been treated to the righteous rollers that AMC conjured up for our delectation during the golden era of large-living, which lasted from roughly 1965 to 1978.

American Motors Corporation may have descended from Hudson and Nash—brands whose hallmarks were modesty and efficiency—but by the mid-1960s, AMC began producing battlewagons of truly Bismarckian proportions.

One of the most memorable of these lunkers was the Ambassador series—AMC's top-of-the-line and fullest-figured car. It was offered in hardtop coupe, sedan, and station wagon forms, and by 1965, it had become AMC's ultimate pavement crusher. When armed with the company's equally mighty 401 V-8, it owned the road like few others before or since.

The upsizing began in 1965 when the all-new Ambassador appeared. Designed by Richard Teague, it rode on a 116-inch wheelbase—an uptick of several inches over the Classic with which it shared sheetmetal DNA. This was still considered modest at the time, but by modern standards, it was already limousine-like. (For some perspective, the wheelbase of a 2010 Mercedes-Benz E-Class sedan measures a puny 112.4 inches.)

Vertical stacked headlights and a wall-to-wall grille gave the car a formal but modern appearance.

In 1966, a minor facelift—revised roofline on hardtop coupes, vertical wraparound taillights, and simulated wood trim for wagons—updated the car's look. A new DPL (for Diplomat) hardtop coupe entered the lineup. DPL coupes and convertibles offered houndstooth interior trim with matching throw pillows and fold-down center armrests along with an available console-mounted four-speed manual gearbox and Twin Grip limited slip rear end.

AMC consisted of a bunch of minor auto manufacturers mostly known for building small, economical cars. The Ambassador's job description was to change that perception.

American Motors stressed
the Bacchanalian qualities of its
Ambassador series in company
advertising.

Opposite: **The Ambassador**
might have been the most staid
model in AMC's staid lineup, but
it still had the nerve to go topless
on occasion.

But this was just the beginning of Big.

By 1967, the Ambassador's wheelbase was extended another two-plus-size
inches, all the way up to 118. Yet the Ambassador was still a *relative* flyweight. Even
wagons (which shared the same 118-inch wheelbase) didn't quite hit 3,200 pounds—
comparable to a modern mid-size car. The DPL hardtop coupe weighed a semisvelte
3,056 pounds.

With the optional high-compression 270-horsepower 327 V-8, performance
was thus quite respectable—even if gas mileage wasn't. A lower-performance (250
horsepower) version of the 327 V-8 was also available, as well as a smaller, 287-cubic-
inch V-8 and AMC's own 232-cubic-inch Typhoon in-line six.

AMC's optional Twin Stick overdrive transmission improved fuel economy by
cutting engine revs at highway speeds. At the time—when premium leaded flowed
like water—no one much cared about fuel efficiency, so very few people thought the
Twin Stick OD was worth the additional cost. Conventional three-speed manual and
automatic transmissions—as well as four-speed manual gearboxes—were much more
commonly ordered.

Today, finding a mid-'60s Ambassador with the Twin Stick overdrive is most
unusual. Four-speed (manual) cars are also relatively rare.

In 1968, a new SST trim made its debut, with the DPL trim shifting to second-tier
status. Air conditioning became standard equipment in the Ambassador—another
first for AMC. At the time, not even Cadillacs and Lincolns came standard with this
feature, despite being vastly more expensive.

By 1969, SST versions of the Ambassador could be equipped with AMC's muscled-
up 390-cubic-inch V-8, packing 325 horsepower. That year, also, the Ambassador's

In order to compete with the luxury cars offered by Detroit's big three—General Motors, Ford, and Chrysler—American Motors included as standard equipment accessories that its larger rivals only offered as optional equipment.

Opposite: **American Motors** introduced a new, larger, more luxurious car for the 1974 model year. Unfortunately for AMC, this introduction coincided with the Arab oil embargo, which caused gas prices to skyrocket and, in turn, led the car-buying public to reject large, luxurious new automobiles. As a result, the *Ambassador* nameplate died after 48 years of use. The car, however, lived on as the Matador Brougham.

wheelbase grew to a truly titanic 122 inches—nearly matching the long-wheelbase version of the final generation of Lincoln's Town Car, which spaced its wheels 123.7 inches apart. And the long-wheelbase Lincoln was an honest-to-goodness limousine, while the Ambassador was just a regular passenger car.

It may have shared dimensions with a limo, but the Ambassador, though exceptionally well appointed, was comparatively inexpensive. A '70 SST, for example, stickered out at a very Middle American $3,739—far less than an equivalent car from GM, Ford, or Chrysler.

With ever-growing length came ever-increasing heft, and by the '71 model year, the Ambassador sedan tipped the scales at well over 3,500 pounds—heavier than the '66 convertible coupe by about 100 pounds. The stately SST wagon had bulked up to 4,000 pounds.

To get all this steel moving, more cubic inches under the hood were urgently needed—and so the '71 Ambassador fielded AMC's largest-ever V-8, the 401. Its rated 330 horsepower was actually 10 horsepower off the mark of the 1970 390 V-8—on paper, at least. (The early '70s were a time of juggling and fudging when it came to advertised horsepower—and published claims are often widely off the mark.) But what the bigger engine may have lacked in high-rpm horsepower it more than made up for with an endless supply of tire-frying low-end torque. If you were a high schooler in those days and had access to Dad's 401 Ambassador, few of your friends could challenge your crown as Burnout King.

Smaller 360 and 304 V-8s were still available, too.

In 1971, a new, luxury-themed Brougham trim was added. The intent was to equal top-of-the-line cars from GM, Ford, and Chrysler on *content*, while undercutting them on *price*. The strategy was effective and sales were strong that year—helped in part by healthy sales to law enforcement, which grew to appreciate the Ambassador's generous legroom.

And its hairy 401 V-8.

In 1972, the six-cylinder engine was dropped from the lineup, and all Ambassadors came equipped with V-8 engines—as well as a new 12-month/12,000-mile bumper-to-bumper warranty. Nineteen seventy-three was the final year for the SST—and all Ambassadors were built with the formerly optional top-of-the-line Brougham trim.

In 1974, a final redesign added another several inches to the car in order to comply with the federal government's new bumper-impact standards. Unfortunately, this added weight at just the moment when impending emissions regulations were forcing automakers to depower their engines. This hurt Ambassador's performance and mileage—and not long thereafter, its sales.

First to feel the heat was the Ambassador coupe, which last saw the light of day in 1973. The sedan and wagon lasted until 1975, when the then intermediate-size Matador series became AMC's biggest car.

Underappreciated and often overlooked by the classic car hobby for the past couple of decades, these beasts could be on the verge of a renaissance today. Excellent condition examples can still be found for well under $10,000—which by the standards of today's old car hobby is a steal.

Ambassador: Things to Know

Ambassador is one of the longest-lived nameplates in automotive history; it was in continuous use from 1927 (under Nash) all the way through to 1974, when production ended.

Ambassador wagons had flat-folding seats that created a sleeping area inside the car.

Equipped with the optional high-compression Rebel V-8, an Ambassador sedan was capable of reaching 60 miles per hour in under 10 seconds and running the quarter-mile in the high 16-second range.

With the Twin Stick overdrive and six-cylinder engine, a mid-'60s Ambassador delivered a respectable-for-the-era 20 miles per gallon on the highway.

Ambassador was one of the first American cars to replace push-button door handles with the paddle-type handles still in use today.

BUICK'S BIG BERTHA
ELECTRA 225
1959-1984

The Buick Electra 225 4-door Hardtop

The Buick Electra 225 4-door Sedan

The Buick Electra 225 Convertible

Historically, Buick was GM's "discreet Cadillac"—a high-end car without the high-end ostentation. For many years, Buicks were known as doctors' cars for just that reason. Ownership indicated you had money, but weren't looking to *flaunt* it.

Like GM's Oldsmobile and Chevrolet divisions, Buick was named after an actual person, its founder—David Dunbar Buick, who emigrated from Scotland as a child with his parents in the early 1850s.

Historians date the first Buick to 1903. Five years later, in 1908, Buick was building more cars (8,000 or so in total) than Ford Motor Company and Cadillac *combined*.

By the mid-1920s, the company was selling more than a quarter-million cars annually.

For decades after its incorporation into the GM family, Buick—also like other GM divisions—operated as a semi-autonomous company. It had its own, in-house engineering department that produced Buick-specific engines that made Buicks more than just rebadged GM generic cars.

These engines—especially the overhead valve nailhead V-8 in Wildcat, Super Wildcat, and GS variants—were among the most powerful engines fielded by an American automaker in their day.

Though younger readers may think of today's Buick as a purveyor of dowdy sedans for the senior citizen set, the truth is that during the company's salad days in the late 1950s, 1960s, and through the mid- to late 1970s, it produced some of the most stylistically daring and physically impressive machines ever to come out of Detroit—or anywhere else.

Like the designers working for Virgil Exner over at Chrysler, the designers at Buick experimented with odd geometric shapes in the early 1960s.

Opposite: **General Motors** redesigned its entire fleet of sedans for the 1965 model year, replacing the flexible X-frames with stout full-perimeter frames. This made a convertible version of the Electra 225 a much more rational proposition.

The Electra 225 was available as a convertible right from the beginning.

The "deuce and a quarter" was Buick's ultimate ship of the line—measuring nearly 19 feet long (225 inches) from snout to tail. This road titan's wheelbase would eventually stretch to a full-figured 127 inches (in 1970), a girth exceeded in the modern era only by six-figure exotic land yachts, such as the Rolls-Royce Phantom or Daimler Maybach. A 2009 Lincoln Town Car's wheelbase registers 117.7 inches, or nearly a *foot* less than the battlewagon Electra's.

Just for some perspective.

The behemoth was originally available as a six-window hardtop sedan, lead sled coupe, and convertible coupe. Like the World War II Iowa class battleships, the 225 outlasted the era it was born in by decades—continuing in production until 1984, until the last of them was finally retired. (The Electra *name* was continued through 1990, but the models built after 1984 were all downsized, front-drive models that ought to be considered distant kin, at best.)

As Buick's flagship model, the 225 offered the best of everything, including one of the first production applications of supplemental restraint systems—air bags, in modern lingo. These became available in 1974, along with Buick's Max Trac traction control system—both of them literally 10–15 years before other cars began to offer such technology.

Electra 225 Custom Convertible.

Of course, a tank as slab-sided as the 225 had little real need for additional safety equipment. Physics is your friend when you're packing two tons of mass, have a hood made of heavy-gauge stamped steel that weighs more than the entire front end of a Honda Civic CVCC, and a bumper that could serve as a girder for the Golden Gate Bridge.

Few ordinary cars stood a chance of surviving an encounter with a 225.

The '65 pillarless hardtop managed to be graceful despite its massive size—in the same way the *Titanic* was a thing of awe-inspiring grace. It took time to run your eyes across the acres of metal and seemingly endless details—from the slatted, slim-line horizontal brake/parking light combo out back to the baroque but handsome chrome touches up front. Electras were among the first of GM's cars to feature hidden wiper blades that tucked under a slightly raised lip at the rear of the hood, a design touch that cleaned up the exterior noticeably even if it did make it a bit harder to clear ice and snow on a cold winter morning.

Though the 225 shared its basic platform with the Oldsmobile 98 (and equivalent Cadillac), the Buick maintained its uniqueness through styling and what was under the hood. Huge V-8s designed and built by Buick—starting with the 401 in 1959 and achieving ultimate expression in 1970, when the 7.4-liter 455-cubic-inch V-8 arrived

The convertible version of the Electra 225 made its final appearance for the 1970 model year. With air conditioning becoming increasingly common, especially on luxury cars like the Electra, convertibles were rapidly losing popularity.

The late 1960s marked the zenith for General Motors automobiles. Difficulties meeting emissions regulations, crippling strikes that began in 1970, and general idiocy in corporate management precipitated a decline that would eventually drive the company into bankruptcy and force a government bailout.

The inside of an Electra offers something that's very welcome in today's world: good old peace and quiet.

In the race to create the plushest, cushiest, crushed-velouriest interior on the market, U.S. automakers jettisoned any pretext of offering anything resembling lateral support.

on the scene—assured the 225 never lacked for thrust.

To Buick's eternal credit, even the last of the 225s were still impressively large—riding on a still-substantial (for the time) 118.9-inch wheelbase. Somewhat confusingly, by this time, Buick had been using the Electra designation as more or less a trim package on other large Buicks, such as the Park Avenue, Limited, and Estate Wagon.

Nineteen eighty was actually the last year that Electra *225* appears in the literature—a quiet admission by Buick of the car's downsizing. The process had actually begun three years earlier, when the Electra's overall length was chopped back by nearly a foot.

Still, like the Pontiac Trans Am of the same period—which still offered bigger engines and better performance than just about anything else then available—the Electra tried to maintain its dignity. Arguably, it succeeded. The Electra 225 (and the plain old—and slightly smaller—Electra) carried the big car flag during an era of size-attrition, when virtually all formerly full-size American cars got squeezed down to the dimensions of what, in better times, would have been considered medium-size cars at best—and compacts at worst.

Inside the Electra

Discover luxury. Spacious elegance. Yours to enjoy. The 1971 Electra 225 Custom Limited and Electra 225 Sport Coupes share the same spacious interior dimensions.
Front head room: 38.8 inches; Rear head room: 38.1 inches; Front leg room: 42.6 inches; Rear leg room: 39.3 inches; Front shoulder room: 64.3 inches; Rear shoulder room: 61.5 inches. (Note: Electra 225 Sport Coupes interior and exterior dimensions are approximations in inches.)

(The 1971 Electra 225 Sport Coupe is not shown in this catalog. Your Buick dealer will be pleased to review its availability with you.)

Outside the Electra

Classic styling. Distinctive. Electra in every exciting inch. The 1971 Electra 225 Sport Coupes are an expression of truly sophisticated luxury automobiles. Length: 226.2 inches; Width: 79.7 inches; Height: 54.4 inches; Wheelbase: 127.0 inches.

Electra Performance

Magnificence in motion. Performance to believe in. Yours to command.

Standard engine: 455-4 V8; Compression Ratio: 8.5:1; Displacement: 455 C.I.D.; Carburetion: 4-barrel.

Transmission: 3-speed Turbo Hydra-matic 400 Automatic Transmission.

Rear Axle Ratio: 2.73. Consult your Buick dealer for information on available ratios.

Electra Comfort

Convenience. Unlimited luxury. Comfort is yours in Electra: New Full-Flo ventilation system; custom full-foam seats; heater and defroster; deluxe steering wheel; electric clock; interior trunk light; smoking set; rear compartment ash trays; front and rear arm rests; Magic-Mirror exterior finish; side coat hooks; door-operated interior light; plus all the interior appointments you've come to expect from Electra.

Electra Special Features

Consider the features you would like to enjoy in a luxury automobile. Electra has them all: 3-speed Turbo Hydra-matic 400 Transmission; variable ratio power steering; self-adjusting power front disc brakes with composite cast iron rear drum brakes; 6,000 mile lubed front suspension; Buick's Accu-Drive with forward mounted steering gear and linkage; direct-acting hydraulic shock absorbers; J78 x 15 bias-belted tires; Delcotron generator; Full-Flow oil filter; remote control outside rear view mirror; four-way hazard warning flasher; radio antenna concealed in the windshield; side guard beam construction for added protection; safety door latches and hinges; padded, energy absorbing instrument panel; newly designed instrument cluster for easier serviceability; semi-closed cooling system that should never overheat, even with air-conditioning; foam padded front head restraints; anti-theft key warning buzzer; anti-theft steering column lock; time modulated carburetor choke control for faster starts in any weather; new evaporative emission control system; four jet windshield washers.

Some of the equipment shown or described is available at extra cost.

Electra 225 Custom Sport Coupe.

Electra 225: Things to Know

As Buick's top-of-the-line model, the Electra 225 boasted four portholes (or Venti-Ports) on its fenders. These, however, were altered during the 1981 model year when pressed-in slats on the side trim were substituted.

Big-bosomed film star and Howard Hughes squeeze Jayne Mansfield died in a '66 Electra.

While models built up to the mid-'70s had Buick-built engines, later '70s models sometimes came equipped with the Oldsmobile-built 403 and 307 V-8s.

A 1959 Electra 225 had an MSRP of $4,192. A 1984 Electra Limited's MSRP was nearly triple that at $13,155.

The longest-overall Electras measured 233.3 inches (in 1976), with the added sheet metal grafted on in order to help the car comply with the federal government's new bumper-impact requirements.

The already gigantic Electra 225 grew even larger for 1971. The car's wheelbase remained an *Edmund Fitzgerald* like 127 inches, but overall length grew to 233 inches. That's 7 inches shy of 20 feet. A Volkswagen Beetle could fit in its trunk. Almost.

HEAVY CHEVY
IMPALA
1958-1996

IMPALA—excitement on wheels

Chevy's new gull-wing fender styling lends an air of soaring grace, luxurious width. Impalas are daringly low, more than seventeen feet long! They feature triple taillight grouping—dual tail lamps, back-up lamp, stop and directional signals—all integrally styled. You can be proud to be seen in it . . . it's the prettiest rear view on the road.

THE IMPALA CONVERTIBLE
IN ONYX BLACK

THE IMPALA SPORT COUPE INTERIOR

In Luxury Lounge interiors you get wall-to-wall luxury, tailored in the most beguiling new colors a car ever wore . . . supple vinyls . . . gaily textured fabrics . . . panels in hues of anodized aluminum. There's a hideaway armrest in the Impala rear seat, and front seat armrests have built-in reflectors to warn oncoming cars when the doors are opened.

THE IMPALA SPORT COUPE
IN SILVER BLUE AND SNOWCREST WHITE

Newest heartthrob in sight—the Impala Sport Coupe. *Longer* by over
nine inches, *lower* by more than two, the Impala, like every '58 Chevy,
wears the look of a car just naturally born for the road. Begin at its
massive new grille and multiple roadlights . . . sweep your glance
along its taut, sleek length. This is the *newest*—that's for sure!

In "modern times," roughly defined as the post-1980s, a low-priced car is almost by definition a *puny* car. The Masses of today are no longer allowed to Live Large.

This was not always so, however.

During the wonder years of America's postwar greatness, working- and middle-class Americans got to drive cars that were longer, bigger, and heavier than the typical $50,000 "luxury" sedan of today—often with even bigger V-8s as standard equipment that produced as much as 425 horsepower. They featured right-wheel drive, too (that is *rear* wheel drive), as well as body-on-frame construction—and could take out a Honda with no more than a scuff on the fender to show for it.

And yet they were inexpensive—in some cases, literally the most affordable cars on the market.

Joe Sixpack never had it so good—and Chevrolet was his brand of choice.

A generation of Americans grew up with TV shows like *Mutual of Omaha's Wild Kingdom*, watching awestruck as great loping beasts like the African impala effortlessly bounded away from predators. Someone at Chevrolet (reportedly, designer Robert Cadaret) may have been watching, too—and realized the graceful, deerlike beast would arouse positive associations in the minds of car buyers.

As the top car in Chevrolet's lineup, the Impala was available with the top engine the division offered—the 348-cubic-inch "big-block," the predecessor of the 409.

Opposite: **When Chevrolet** introduced the Impala for the 1958 model year, it was the top model in the division's lineup, a prestige car for the average American.

While early 1960s Chevrolet Impalas have proven popular with the low-rider community, their weak X-frame chassis poorly suited them for hydraulic jumping suspension systems. They didn't need hydraulic systems to do acrobatics, though; the frames on these cars would wind up and jump while the cars were driving down billiard-table-smooth roads.

Thus was born the first four-wheeled Impala, in 1958.

Conceived initially as a high-trimmed Bel Air, by 1959 Impala had become a distinct model series within Chevy's lineup. In the beginning, coupe, convertible, and sedan versions were available. All featured more chrome, nicer interiors—and room for six.

Impala would prove immensely popular with buyers, partially because of the attractive styling—which for 1959 included a wicked-looking pair of arches that began near the doors and met up in a pleated V over the trunk lid of the coupe. Slinky-looking cat's-eye taillights were another daring styling touch.

Overall length had grown by nearly a foot, too—and width by seven inches. Impala had grown into a very full-figured gal indeed.

But the core reason for Impala's success was the high value for the dollar it offered buyers. While Chevrolet was GM's entry-level brand and very much a working man's car in the late 1950s and early 1960s, the Impala offered the working man the opportunity to drive a car that stacked up very favorably against GM's more costly Pontiac, Oldsmobile, and Buick models—as well as competitors from Ford and elsewhere.

For example, there was the brilliant OHV small-block V-8 engine—the step-up option over the standard Blue Fame in-line six. The compact, lightweight, and high-powered V-8 was an engineering tour de force, not just for its time, but for all time.

It was based on an oversquare (larger bore than stoke) layout with five main bearings, lightweight aluminum slipper pistons (for high-RPM capability), and forged steel crankshaft (for strength at high RPMs), and it boasted a modern, high-pressure oiling system, among other innovations. The engine was made with room to grow, and within a few years of its introduction in 1955, the little V-8 was producing more than one horsepower for each cubic inch of its displacement (in Power Pak form). It would remain in regular production well into the twenty-first century with only minor changes to its basic design.

Engineer Ed Cole called it a "blue sky" engine—a once-in-a-lifetime opportunity to design something from scratch. And to get it *right*. That it lasted in serial production well into the following century is irrefutable evidence of its greatness.

Buyers of the "humble" Chevy thus got a powerplant that was one of the finest engines available at the time, if not all time. And it came in a car that cost only about $2,700 (in 1959), which meant it was a true Everyman's Car.

In addition to the impressive powerplant, early Impalas also had prestigious underthings—in that they shared a modified version of the same basic frame with higher-priced cars from Buick, Oldsmobile, and even Cadillac.

By late 1959—a little more than one year out of the gate—Chevy sold more than 400,000 of them. *Millions* would find homes over the coming decades—helping Chevrolet become "USA-1" literally (in terms of total sales), as well as figuratively (as far as fans were concerned).

In addition to the sturdy and economical but otherwise unremarkable Blue Flame Six and the enthusiastic new 283 V-8, Impala buyers could also select either of two heavy-hitting Turbo Thrust big-block V-8s. The 348 four-barrel began at 250 horsepower and could be outfitted with performance camshaft and other upgrades all the way up to 335 horsepower.

The high-value, high-trim Impala was quickly becoming high-powered, too.

In 1961, Chevy threw down the gauntlet—unveiling the first Impala Super Sport. The centerpiece of the SS package would quickly become another legend in its own right—the 409 big-block V-8.

This muscular mountain motor delivered 7-second 0–60 times and low 15-second quarter-mile runs. The Beach Boys sang an ode to the fearsome Impala SS— "She's so fine, my 409!"—that, like the car, quickly became a hit. Drivers of lesser cars became very familiar with the Impala's signature six taillights.

With a full-perimeter frame, the 1965 Impala represented a dramatic improvement over its X-framed predecessor. This was the beginning of a golden era for General Motors, a period in which the company produced what could well have been the best automobiles in the world at that time.

Impala Super Sport . . . *personalized version of Chevrolet's most elegant series*—Chevrolet's special Impala Super Sport equipment* gives you a unique opportunity to combine sports car style and features with full-size room and comfort. It is available for both the Impala Sport Coupe and Impala Convertible and includes: front bucket seats; leather-soft vinyl throughout; sports car assist bar; between-seat console with locking compartment; patterned aluminum body side molding insert; wheel covers with knock-off hub styling; plus distinctive Super Sport identification. You can gear up the go to match the sporty look with Chevrolet's many performance options*. Choose from one of Chevrolet's four optional V8's (ranging from 250 h.p. to 409 h.p.) and such high-performance equipment as 4-Speed Synchro-Mesh transmission, sintered-metallic brake linings, heavy-duty springs and shocks, 8.00 x 14 tires and electric tachometer.

Optional at extra cost.

In the early 1960s the family sedans from Ford and Chevy were fairly rationally sized. They were just big enough to hold Mom, Dad, and four to six kids. Of course, kids were much smaller in those days, back before they suckled all day on sugary soda pop.

The SS wasn't all about the engine, though. Also included were numerous functional and cosmetic upgrades, from a tough-looking engine-turned aluminum dash trim plate to an optional tachometer, sintered metallic brake shoes, heavy-duty suspension, wider wheels and tires, and a floor-shifted four-speed manual gearbox. A two-speed Powerglide automatic was also available—and became a popular tool for drag racers (who never needed third gear before they reached the traps at the end of the quarter-mile).

It was a hairy-looking beast—with its insolently arched-up trunk lid and provocative side-panel swoosh.

Though it had the performance *curriculum vitae* of a muscle car, the full-size Impala SS was bigger and heavier than most intermediate-size street maulers like the Chevy II and Chevelle. Its coil-sprung suspension was also smoother than the truck-derived leaf spring/solid axle setup that was more commonly found underneath muscle car intermediates, which gave it a luxury touch few of the more highly distilled muscle cars could equal.

The Impala SS was—and remains—a brooding presence that's more at home sauntering along menacingly, driver low in the seat, Raybans set just right, than it is dragging down the quarter-mile.

After all, when you're big you don't need to run.

Others run from *you.*

Chevy turned the page a bit beginning with the 1971 restyle, which was less rumbly muscle car—and more Big Bertha. She still packed a punch, though—so you didn't want to make fun of her meaty forearms or ruddy cheeks.

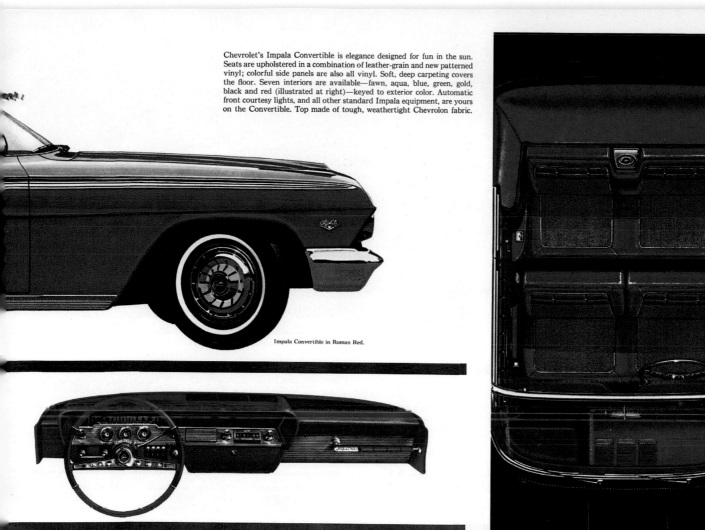

Chevrolet's Impala Convertible is elegance designed for fun in the sun. Seats are upholstered in a combination of leather-grain and new patterned vinyl; colorful side panels are also all vinyl. Soft, deep carpeting covers the floor. Seven interiors are available—fawn, aqua, blue, green, gold, black and red (illustrated at right)—keyed to exterior color. Automatic front courtesy lights, and all other standard Impala equipment, are yours on the Convertible. Top made of tough, weathertight Chevrolon fabric.

Impala Convertible in Roman Red.

While most other manufacturers gave their cars tailfins of cartoonish proportions in the late 1960s, Chevrolet designers kept their fins subdued and elegant.

The new Impala shared its chassis and basic platform with other GM B-body full-size cars, such as the Pontiac Parisienne, and rode on an Olympian 121.5-inch wheelbase—Chevy's largest (except for wagons). The sedan weighed more than 4,000 pounds fully tanked up and with its driver aboard—and appropriately offered the latest, largest version of Chevy's big-block V-8, displacing 454 cubic inches.

A short-lived small-block 400 V-8 was also available but, due to overheating issues resulting from its siamesed bores, did not last long in production.

While the SS package was no more, Chevy did offer some sport-themed Impalas during the mid-'70s, including a Spirit of America Sport Coupe for 1974, which had special red, white, and blue trim; Rally wheels and outside mirrors (similar to those used on Camaro); and a color-keyed vinyl top. In 1975, a similar Landau package replaced the Spirit of America package. It centered on the vinyl roof (more color options) and exterior/interior trim enhancement. It became a popular upgrade during the disco era.

The 1977–1979 models also had a neat-looking and very unusual modified fastback rear glass section (shared with the Caprice), defined by bent ends that must have been extremely challenging to mass produce.

Chevy created some confusion when it introduced the Caprice as a companion model in the mid-1960s. It was initially supposed to be an upper-trimmed Impala—though, of course, the Impala itself was originally conceived as a high-trimmed version of the Bel Air.

Yes, the lovely blonde in the ad could fit all that junk in the trunk of her Impala. Snoop around in there, and you might find a dozen clowns hidden in the various nooks and crannies, along with a stray Shriner or two.

You get room in a Big Chevrolet.

Head room
Sit up tall. Head high. Be proud.
You're thinking of buying a Chevrolet.
And if you do you'll be able to do all those things. (There's head room for most any six-footer, plus. Plus hat.)

Shoulder room
Whatever shape your shoulders are in, there's room for yours and five more pairs in the sedans or four more in the other Big Chevrolets.
It's a nice feeling.

Hip room
You'll also find there's enough room in sedans for all six people to be 42 inches around—room for five in coupes and the convertible.
How many people do you know that are 42 inches around?

Leg room
Your legs stretch out in front of you when you sit in a Chevrolet.
No scrunching them off to one side.
No tucking them under your chin.
No knocking your knees on the instrument panel. Try a test stretch for size.
It's tremendous.

Trunk room
You can pack what you need.
What you think you may need.
And what you won't need, but plan to take along anyway. You've got about 18 cubic feet for it.

14

Chevrolet Impala 4-Door Sedan

Five variations. Each a better way in its own way.

IMPALA SPORT SEDAN ▲

▼ IMPALA 4-DOOR SEDAN

▲ IMPALA SPORT COUPE

BEL AIR 4-DOOR SEDAN ▼

▲ IMPALA CONVERTIBLE

We'll let the pictures do most of the talking. They can help you settle on what you might settle in much faster than words alone can.

Just keep in mind that all the Impalas you see here have all the important Impala features we've talked about.

And keep in mind Bel Air.

Now don't get the idea it's an Impala that didn't quite make it.

Bel Air is Bel Air. It's its own car. With a lot of reasons for taking a close look at it.

Like power steering, yes. Automatic transmission with any V8, yes. Power disc brakes up front, yes. A sound-absorbing double-panel roof, sure. Plus a refined flow-through power ventilation system.

But Bel Air has one feature all its own going for you. Its very low Chevrolet price.

Impala Landau Custom Coupe.

Impala Custom Coupe.

Impala 4-Door Sedan. Available options featured are body side molding, wheel opening mouldings, wheel covers, white stripe tires, deluxe bumpers and bumper guards.

Impala Sport Sedan. Available options shown are wheel covers, white stripe tires, deluxe bumpers and bumper guards.

Chevrolet appeared to be at the top of its game in the early 1970s. Its sedans defined the American automobile—an advertising campaign of the period touted, "Baseball, hot dogs, apple pie, and Chevrolet." But behind the scenes, the chaos caused by UAW strikes and the technical requirements of meeting upcoming emissions and safety regulations were sowing the seeds of the company's eventual bankruptcy.

Left: **Like General Motors'** other large sedans, the Impala grew to Leviathan-like proportions by 1976. But families were getting smaller, gas was getting more expensive, and people were increasingly turning to smaller cars.

Chevrolet revived both the *SS* and the *Impala* names for the final generation of the rear-wheel-drive version car. To create the Impala SS, the division simply applied the police package to the civilian Caprice Classic, which had replaced the Impala entirely in the 1980s.

As the years passed, there was often much in common between Caprice and Impala—so much so, in fact, that by the early '80s it was sometimes hard to tell which was which. By the Reagan years, the Impala had become the grocery getter/rental car/cop-mobile—while the higher-trimmed Caprice took over as the nice version of the car driven by civilians.

In 1985, the Impala name itself was temporarily retired—though the Caprice lived on through 1996.

A temporary resurrection of the Impala's former greatness occurred in the early '90s, when GM brought back both the Impala nameplate and the Impala's big car *bona fides*. While some critics mocked the new car as Shamu because of its piscine proportions and curves, it was exactly the kind of car regular Americans used to have access to in the '50s and '60s and '70s—but which had largely disappeared by the late 1980s as federal fuel-economy standards killed off traditionally sized American cars.

The SS package was also revived—with Corvette power (in the form of a 260-horsepower LT1 350 cubic-inch V-8) under the hood, a neatly done stylized Impala leaper badge, fat 17-inch rims, and the whole car done up in tuxedo black.

Other colors became available, too—but *black* was always this car's best color.

It was, unfortunately, a short-lived reprieve. GM dropped the SS Impala soon after 1996, even though demand was still strong. The reason for the decision was simply that GM wanted to use the Arlington, Texas, plant where Impalas were assembled for trucks and SUVs instead. That decision spelled the end for what was arguably America's last family-size—and family-priced—big-engined, big car.

Subsequent Impalas were destined to be exclusively front-wheel drive and barely matched the exterior/interior dimensions of an old Nova or Chevy II. It wasn't the same—even when Chevy added V-8 power and (once again) resurrected the SS package.

When it comes to a car named Impala, size *does* matter.

Impala: Things to Know

The Impala has been one of GM's most successful car lines, with annual sales approaching half a million in peak years.

The '69 SS 427 Impala is the most potent of all the SS Impalas, with 425 horsepower on tap.

Mid-1970s Impalas offered an EconoMinder gauge package to help owners maximize fuel efficiency. The system centered on a dashboard gauge that translated engine vacuum levels into "instant" MPG readings.

GM built right-hand-drive versions of the Impala for the export market.

In the 1990s, Shamu-the-whale versions of the Impala were a very popular choice for law enforcement and taxi fleets.

UPSCALE BREAD AND BUTTER
CHEVROLET CAPRICE
1965-1996

Choose any Jet-smooth 1966 Chevrolet. It'll be well built, comfortable, dependable and good looking . . . like the new Caprice Custom Coupe above with its one-of-a-kind roof line.

The most luxurious Chevrolet yet built—now in four models

Caprice '66

From 1965 through the mid-1990s, the Chevy Caprice was marketed as the nicer version of the Impala. In subsequent years, there would be some overlap between the two—and in fact, in the final years, the Impala (in SS form) actually swapped places with the Caprice, becoming the nicer (and often, higher-powered) version.

But originally, Caprice was intended to be Chevy's Cadillac—a full-size car fitted out with a top-of-the-line interior and trim upgrades—fancy wheel covers, plush vinyl or cloth seats with fold-down armrests, extra-deep carpets, vanity lights, and (in later years) vinyl-covered roofs very much like what you'd expect on a higher-priced Cadillac—all of it priced within reach of the working man. In 1965, for example, a Caprice-optioned Impala sedan with a 283 V-8 cost about $2,800.

By 1965, people had become used to the Impala version of the Chevrolet sedan. The division needed an even more upscale version, so it introduced the Caprice Classic, distinguished from the Impala by its formal roofline in place of the sportier Impala's fastback design.

Chevrolet Caprice Sedan

Buyers responded favorably; more than 800,000 Impalas were sold that year—many of these optioned with the new Caprice package.

To keep up the momentum—and also to provide the Caprice with more in the way of its own identity—in '66 Chevy changed the sheet metal, giving the Caprice (but not the Impala) a more squared-off, formal roofline that contrasted with the regular Impala coupe's fastback look. V-8 power became standard equipment, too. A wagon was added to the lineup this year as well—giving Caprice buyers three different ways to go.

Unusual equipment included an early form of automatic climate control air conditioning very similar to the system found in a Cadillac. It was marketed by Chevy as Comfortron AC, and it automatically maintained a driver-set temperature regardless of the season—as opposed to the more clumsy cold and hot settings used in many early AC systems. A tilt and telescoping wheel was also available. Both features were large-living items for a mere Chevy—and also for the mid-1960s, when such features were still considered indulgences of the affluent.

Prices ranged from just under $3,000 for a coupe to $3,347 for a wagon with three rows of seats and a 283 or 327 V-8 under the hood. More than 181,000 were sold during the '66 run—making Caprice one of Chevy's most popular new entrants.

But the true Birth of Bigness would take place five years later, in 1971, when the all-new Caprice—riding on an enlarged 121.5-inch wheelbase—rolled out of the Arlington, Texas, plant where all Caprices were born. This car had elegant-looking rear wheel skirts, formal quarter windows, and a flight deck of a hood that was very much Caddy comparable. So too was the deep-breathing egg-crate grille up front—

In the early 1970s, General Motors relied heavily on badge engineering—that is, they added a few luxury features (maybe a vinyl top and a set of fender skirts) and called a car a new model, the formula used to create the Caprice Classic. This worked as long as there was no real competition from abroad, but when the Japanese invasion began at the end of the decade, GM found that it was just slicing thinner and thinner pieces from the same pie.

Opposite: **Chevrolet marketed** the Caprice as an upscale version of the Impala sedan. While it was certainly more luxurious than the Impala or other lesser Chevrolets, it was still a step down from a Buick, Oldsmobile, or Cadillac.

Caprice Classic Landau Coupe.

Caprice Classic Coupe.

Caprice Classic 4-Door Sedan.

Caprice Classic Sport Sedan.

which gave the car a toothsome countenance. Battering ram bumpers completed the effect. Inside, buyers could select a Comfort Custom steering wheel, Stratobench seats with fold-down armrests, and wood trim.

Turbo-Jet 454 big-block V-8 power was the icing on the cake. Three-hundred-sixty horsepower under your right foot. High-beam button for the quad headlights to your left. Endlessly tough Turbo-Hydra 400 three-speed automatic ready for power braking—and even neutral dropping—tire-frying launches.

Teenagers of the time who were lucky enough to snatch some seat time faced a mile-wide horizontal speedo with large numerals stretched to each end of the breadbox dash. The numbers bunched up in the middle but began to cant to the right as road speed increased. Sixty, seventy, eighty, ninety miles per hour. Hunter S. Thompson gave a memorable account of running an early '70s Caprice convertible ("the shark") at top speed through the Nevada desert while high on a variety of illegal substances. These colossal Chevys were hell on wheels in a straight line, but take a curve at anything much above the posted maximum and usually at least two of the car's wheel covers would fly off into the ditch to mark your passing.

Like an old sun expanding to its red giant stage, Caprice grew even larger for 1975 and 1976—though wheelbase remained the same 121.5 inches. The beast now measured nearly 223 inches from tip to tip—which was about 5 inches longer overall than the 1971 model.

Weight, too, now topped two tons.

The grille remained wide, but it wasn't as tall, which along with the new squared-off quad headlights gave the Caprice a smug, cat-ate-the-canary look. Full wheel covers, rear skirts, and ever-more-generous interior appointments (including pulse wipers) continued the Caprice's ersatz Cadillac tradition.

The year 1975 would be the last for a convertible Caprice—though the 454 survived, and despite a single exhaust and a stifling catalytic converter, it still managed a solid 235 horsepower. Landau sport mirrors and a color-keyed vinyl roof were on the options list. The 454 went away after 1976—replaced by the 350-cubic-inch (and later, 305) small-blocks that became Caprice mainstays through the final years.

We live in a downsized era, in which few genuinely broad-shouldered boulevardiers roam freely. Thus, while the 1977-1990 Caprice was considered mid-size in its time, by the standards of our time, its 212-inch overall length is as hard to appreciate nowadays as the gold standard or Coke with sugar instead of high-fructose corn syrup in it.

In 1991, Chevrolet unveiled a controversial new

Caprice: Things to Know

A rare option on the '69 Caprice was the liquid tire chain system—which used a driver-actuated spray on the back tires to enhance traction on slick roads.

In 1973, Chevy changed the car's name from just *Caprice* to *Caprice Classic*—which endured through the 1980s.

Ninteen seventy-five was the first year for dual readout speedometers that had both miles per hour and kilometers per hour.

The year 1977 was the first since 1965 that a V-8 engine was not standard equipment in the Caprice.

The 1977–1979 Caprice had a very unusual fastback-style rear glass section that had bent side sections rather than the usual flat or curved single slab.

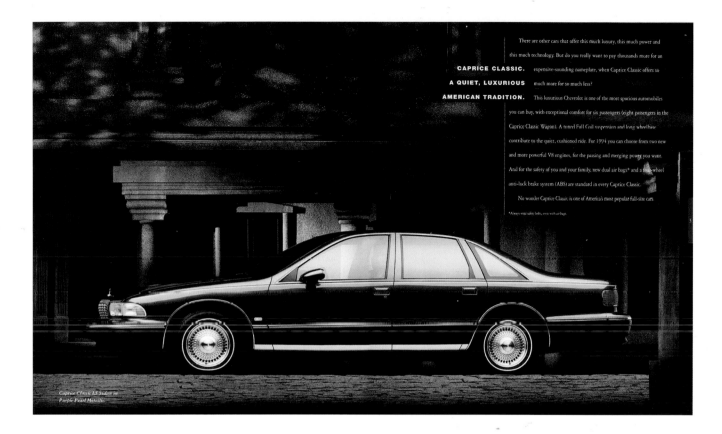

Caprice Classic LS Sedan in Purple Pearl Metallic.

Caprice—which looked like it might have been inspired by a walrus lying on an ice floe. Car reviewers christened it Shamu—after the Sea World whale. It was nearly half a foot longer than the previous Caprice and with nary a straight line or angle to be found. It was a curvaceous sheetmetal belly dancer designed to glide through the wind with six passengers riding in coil-sprung comfort. These latter-day Caprices also boasted Corvette-sourced powerplants in the form of the potent 5.7-liter (350 cube) LT1 V-8, albeit detuned and with some changes, including cast-iron rather than aluminum heads.

Police departments felt a special affection for the Caprice—which had room for multiple offenders in back as well as plentiful legroom up front. As the ranks of rear-drive, V-8-powered sedans thinned to nearly nonexistent, it became one of the most commonly used vehicles for police work in the country. Even after Chevy cancelled the car, it was so beloved by the men in blue that many departments actually paid for complete refurbishments of their aging and tired fleets of Caprices rather than buy a new fleet of Ford Crown Victorias (the only other similar car around). Reason? The Vics had the *room*, but not the *power*—and they didn't handle nearly as well, either.

These Hefty Haulers were among the last survivors of the golden age of the American car—when big cars with big V-8s weren't just for the rich (as they mostly have been since the beginning of the twenty-first century).

In 1997, the Caprice was replaced by the wretched Lumina LTZ—a front-wheel-drive, V-6-powered compact with the cringing mien of a turtle that expects at any moment to be hit over the head with a stick. The plant at Arlington, Texas, was turned over to truck and SUV production—which a few years later would prove to be a foolish decision indeed when the market for SUVs tanked, a major factor in General Motors' bankruptcy.

The Caprice had one final redesign in the 1990s. It was one of the last full-size, rear-wheel-drive, body-on-frame cars ever offered for sale and became a favorite among police departments nationwide. However, like the nanyangosaurus, a dinosaur that was roughly the same size as the final Caprice Classic, it had outlived its eon.

Opposite: **From 1976 on,** you could get your Caprice Classic in just about any configuration, unless you wanted a convertible.

OLDSMOBILE ELEPHANT
REGENCY SEDAN
1971-1984

In public office, you examine issues and alternatives—and try to get the most for each dollar spent. It's exactly the same process I used in choosing my 98 Regency.

NINETY EIGHT REGENCY SEDAN

Oldsmobile seemed to have a fetish for marketing its cars to people in the legal professions, such as judges and lawyers. Today we can see how well that worked out for the division.

Oldsmobile, like Anne Boleyn, probably never actually felt the blade.

By the time the end came in 2002, Oldsmobile was already effectively dead. General Motors had moved on to other tarts, such as Pontiac and Saturn (they too would lose their heads within another few years) and quickly forgot about its former *amore*—the division that had once been a favorite both within and without.

Within, for the money it made the company. *Without*, for the stylish and powerful and often-innovative cars that carried the rocket crest.

Of these, a sky blue or metallic chocolate brown 98 sedan must be acknowledged as a true exemplar of the breed. It may not be *quite* a Cadillac—but it often came pretty damn close.

Oldsmobile's largest road hog was the 98 sedan and its most massive incarnation appeared in 1971—just in time for the first OPEC oil shocks, inflation, and (very shortly thereafter) waning public interest in cars that achieved single-digit gas mileage.

But as the last Hurrah of Hefty, the fifth-generation 98 made no apologies to anyone.

It was true leviathan—pushing 20 feet long from the rocket badge on its nose to the tip of its stubby rear tail fins, which were styled to look Cadillac-esque and also to differentiate the 98 from the lesser-ranked Olds 88, the division's entry-level large sedan—which had no fins at all.

The '71 98 rode on a 127-inch wheelbase—3 inches longer than the 88's—and tipped the scales at an Atlas-squashing 4,533 pounds fully dressed. Standard under the hood was a low-compression version of the Rocket 455 V-8, rated at 225 horsepower under the new SAE net standards that were coming into effect.

Buyers could upgrade to a more powerful version of the 455 with 250 horsepower.

By modern standards, 225–250 horsepower out of a 7.5-liter V-8 may seem a sloppily inefficient use of all those cubic inches. And, of course, it was. Modern engines of a fraction the displacement easily make as much or more horsepower—but what makes all the difference is that you have to *work* those little engines to get it. Cast-iron lunkers like the Olds 455 specialized in diesel-like torque output at extremely low engine rpm. We're talking 350-plus lbs-ft of torque available with the engine barely running at a fast idle—and another 50 on tap if you revved the huge V-8 a few rpms higher. This was just what the Dr. (Dr. Oldsmobile, perhaps?) ordered—when the prescription called for getting all that mass moving.

NINETY-EIGHT REGENCY COUPE

Your personal edition of the "thinking man's luxury car."

Luxury coupes traditionally afford a very personal expression of one's taste and lifestyle in an automobile—and the Regency Coupe for 1977 improves on that tradition in exciting new ways it couldn't before. It starts with a new size, new maneuverability and new fuel economy that are quite remarkable in a full-size luxury car—and can add to your personal enjoyment of driving.

Redesigned instrumentation

Regency reflects your taste in design as well. Sophisticated. But functional. The clean, elegant line. The jeweled details. And you can personalize it further, if you wish, with an available landau roof or leather seats.

Rear seat passengers may be amazed at the way Regency pampers them, too. To enter, they just tilt the front seatback forward—no more latches to grope for. There's more legroom and headroom—and the rear seat is two inches wider than last year. They can lean back on loose-look cushions, tip down the center armrest, and enjoy the view through generously sized opera windows. While you enjoy a new experience in driving.

If you have a personal preference for luxurious living, Regency is for you.

Today, even the sportiest cars like the Mitsubishi Evo and the Subaru WRX STI have four doors, but in the before times, a sporty car had to have no more than two doors. Even an unsporting land yacht like the Oldsmobile 98 Regency Brougham.

In the late 1960s, the list of standard features on Oldsmobile's 98 Regency was second to none, including a 455-cubic-inch Rocket V-8, variable-ratio power steering, a TH 400 automatic transmission, power brakes, power windows, power door locks, and power seats.

And not just moving, but moving easily. The whole object of a top-tier luxury barge back in the early to mid-1970s was gentle, forceful forward progress. And this is what the 455 Rocket was born to deliver, every time the driver eased into the gas pedal. There was no tachometer—such piffle was unnecessary—just a foot-long speedometer with readouts as broad as the V-8's torque curve. An unkillable THM400 three-speed automatic mediated between the 455, your right foot, and the unfortunate pavement beneath the wire-wheeled and whitewall-shod rims. If you so desired, laying 30 yards or more of rubber was one stab of the gas pedal away.

Though the 98 also sold as a coupe, by far the sedan was the sales leader—87,492 sold for 1971 versus 37,564 coupes. Base price for the sedan that year was $4,807—or almost a buck per pound!

Style-wise, the 98 was an interesting counterpoint to the similarly proportioned but less a sheetmetal David Lee Roth than Cadillac's Sedan deVille. It had smoother lines overall and tended to be rounded off where the Caddy was angular. Slight fender flares around the lower rocker panels extended outward to protect the finish against stone chips as well as add some subtle flair. Rear skirts added an elegant touch.

Chrome trim was not excessive—and nothing stuck out or especially called attention to itself.

The whole point, from Oldsmobile's marketing perspective, was to offer buyers a stately and handsome car that wasn't as gaudy as its Cadillac cousin. Also, one that was almost as opulent on the inside.

In addition to pillowed and tufted bench-style seats (with grab handles and storage pouches for rear seat occupants), frameless door glass (power activated, naturally), cruise control, pulse wipers, Tempmatic air conditioning, and electric rear defrost, the 98 was one of the first GM cars (and first cars, period) to offer air bags as optional equipment (in 1974 and continuing through 1976). Oldsmobile marketed these as air cushion restraints—and was asking $700 for them, a big ticket item on a car that carried a base price (in 1974) of $5,303.

Not surprisingly, only a few cars were so equipped—and with 4,500 pounds of mass in your corner, the air bags were hardly necessary. But they were on the menu, nonetheless.

In addition, buyers could upgrade their 98 to Regency status (beginning with the 1972s), a new top-of-the-line trim package that was launched to commemorate the 75th anniversary of Oldsmobile. The package was coordinated with high-end jeweler Tiffany & Company of New York. Each 98 Regency featured a quartz crystal Tiffany clock in the dashboard, Tiffany Gold Paint, pillow effect crushed velour seats—and was also registered at Tiffany's. Even the keys were special. Lost keys could be dropped in any mailbox and would be automatically returned to the owner.

For 1975, Olds added a theft-deterrent system to the options list that flashed the headlights and sounded the horn if a break-in attempt was detected. Backlighting for

98: Things to Know

Convertible coupes had been offered previously but were dropped after the '70 model run ended.

Technically, only the '72 Regencys are also 75th anniversary models; about 2,650 of these were built, according to records.

Model 98s built in 1972 are the only 98s with parking lamps not located in the bumper.

Models from 1974–1976 equipped with the optional air bag system are extremely rare; at most a few hundred of these cars were built since most buyers did not feel the need for the extra expense of the new (and unproven) safety technology.

Seventies-era Oldsmobile ads implied a custom-built touch with the slogan, "Can we build one for you?"

the driver's side door keyhole was incorporated, too—and in keeping with the times, an engine vacuum-based fuel economy gauge was added to the instrument cluster in order that owners could see at a glance how rapidly they were helping to deplete the world's supply of crude oil.

In 1977, Oldsmobile trimmed the fat considerably with the introduction of a new 98 that was almost a foot shorter overall (221.4 inches) and that had lost 8 inches of wheelbase (down to 119 inches) and about 700 pounds. Also gone was the Rocket 455—replaced by the small-block 403 (which was basically a large-bore version of the Oldsmobile 350 V-8). It was still a substantial beast, even so—and retained most of the essentials that made earlier 98s such enjoyable boozy cruisers. The 403 churned out ample low-end grunt, the Prima velour was still pillowy, wire wheels still flew off if you tried to corner too fast—and the trunk was more than large enough to handle a few bodies rolled up in carpet, if you happened to be "connected."

Oldsmobile would continue to tweak the basic 1977 design all the way through the 1984 model year before the changeover to the new front-wheel-drive layout. Olds probably should have done the decent thing and retired the 98 nameplate but chose instead to continue using it on meager pretenders (including a hideous bathtub-styled thing that arose in 1991) that eventually helped put Oldsmobile into the ground for good in 2002.

The Regency interior with divided front seat, front and rear center armrests, and velour upholstery, all standard. Shown in Dark Claret. Sit down, down, down.

REGENCY

Ninety-Eight Regency: Oldsmobile's ultimate full-size luxury car. A new sophistication for the '80s. Traditionally spacious and comfortable. Yet improved in rolling resistance and aerodynamics over last year. And priced substantially less than many of its peers, whether you buy or lease.

(1) Long before this Regency ever hit the test track, its ride qualities had been tested through computer simulation. (2) You can order a glass or metal sliding sunroof. (3) An amazingly accurate digital clock is standard. (4) The interior dress it in crushed velour, white vinyl—or available leather seats (shown).

No brothel ever sported more opulent décor than the rear-wheel-drive Oldsmobile 98 Regency Brougham.

For the complete bordello experience, a buyer could forgo the optional leather interior and stick with the standard-equipment plush velour. The only thing missing was the velvet painting of the boy-child Elvis in the manger.

Next pages: **While the quality** of other GM products suffered in the 1970s and 1980s, the most luxurious models of the various divisions remained well-built automobiles right up until the end.

A night on the town. It takes a special car that fits the mood, the place and the people.

THERE IS A SPECIAL FEEL IN AN OLDSMOBILE

There are those special places and special occasions that demand a special kind of car. The Ninety-Eight Regency Brougham Sedan. Smooth and sophisticated. Thoroughly at ease in fine surroundings. It makes for both a dramatic entrance as well as exit. The next time there's a special affair, look around you. You'll find othe Regency owners enjoying that same feeling of pride.

NINETY-EIGHT REGENCY BROUGHAM SEDAN

5

CHAPTER 3

COUPES de GRACE

Two-Ton Two-Doors

Chrysler Cordoba
Cadillac Coupe de Ville
Buick Riviera
AMC Matador
Chevy Monte Carlo/Laguna

Throughout the 1960s and into the early 1970s, Chrysler Corporation had built its reputation on its Dodge and Plymouth muscle cars, but by the mid-1970s, the muscle-car movement was deader than dead. With the introduction of the Cordoba for the 1975 model year, Chrysler had exactly the right product for the time, and the company sold more than 150,000 units in the first year.

CHRYSLER'S BIGGEST LOSER
CORDOBA 1975-1983

Cordoba instrument panel. The emphasis is on making the driver's job easier.

THE DIMENSIONS OF FUNCTION

Cordoba's instrument panel adds further meaning to its theme of individual elegance. Rich walnut-like inserts are laid over the entire panel surface. Finely-tooled filigree metal edging imparts an elegant detailed effect. Oil pressure, fuel, temperature and alternator gauges and a low-fuel warning light are standard. So is the amazingly accurate electronic digital clock which is canted toward the driver for better viewing. A tachometer makes a most desirable option.

Driving controls are located for easy use. Light and wiper/washer switches and heater/air

Cordoba's optional bucket seat, superbly tailored leather with vinyl trim.

conditioning controls are clustered at the left of the steering column. Cordoba's windshield washers, located on the wiper arm for more efficient cleaning, are standard. The TorqueFlite shift lever is mounted on the steering column, or in the floor-mounted console should you prefer Cordoba's optional bucket seat design. At your left fingertip, you'll welcome the optional Auto Speed Control—an ideal fuel-saving device that automatically steadies and monitors your speed at today's reduced levels.

And the same applies to dozens of other conveniences, described in detail on Pages 6 and 7, with which you can make your Cordoba an even more satisfying experience.

5

How can one discuss the Cordoba without waxing eloquent over the soft Corinthian leather swaddling its interior? Cordoba pitchman Ricardo Montalban later admitted the name *Corinthian* was chosen simply because it sounded elegant when spoken in his Spanish-accented English.

The 1970s were a tough time for fashion—and for Chrysler. Big cars were in the position of an aging, overweight jock trying to make the team for one last season. The size was still there but so were the love handles (in the form of often clumsily tacked-on bumpers put there to meet newly passed federal crashworthiness edicts), and where once beat the heart of a true hero (in the form of 300- and even 400-horsepower V-8s) now sat an arteriosclerotic remnant.

And Chrysler was hit hardest because its specialty had been precisely the kinds of cars that 1970s-era Americans were turning away from. The dilemma was how to sell a big car in a small car environment.

And the solution Chrysler came up with was called Cordoba.

Previous pages: **For 1979** Chrysler tried to revive Cordoba sales by introducing a sporty, upscale 300SE version. The ploy didn't work, but it was a very cool car.

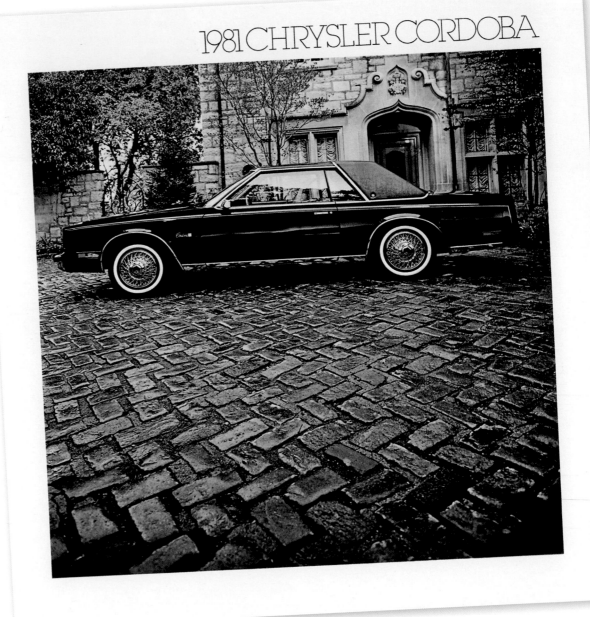

1981 CHRYSLER CORDOBA

In 1980, Chrysler moved the Cordoba to the smaller Aspen/Volare platform. The smaller Cordobas never caught on, and in four years of production, Chrysler sold less than 100,000 of the model. This was in part due to the abysmal throttle-body fuel-injection system used on the 318 V-8 from 1981 until 1983.

Opposite: **Not much changed on the Cordoba** during its first five years in production, other than the round headlights being replaced by pairs of stacked rectangular headlights. Total sales were healthy, nearing 750,000 units by the end of 1979, but as the decade wound down, the Cordoba was starting to show its age.

Ricardo Montalban achieved cultural immortality not for being the genetically enhanced, jump-suited superman Khan on *Star Trek*—or the suave, white-suited Mr. Roark on *Fantasy Island*—but for explaining that his needs were *completely* met by the rich, Corinthian leather-swaddled Chrysler Cor*d*oba.

As for the Cordoba—it may have saved Chrysler, or at least, delayed the collapse (and first government bail-out) that occurred in the early '80s.

Of America's Big Three, Chrysler was hardest hit by the three body blows of the 1970s—the surge in energy costs caused by OPEC, rabid competition from the Japanese (who got an artificial leg up in the U.S. market thanks to the sudden imposition of fuel efficiency mandates that punished the full-size cars that were Chrysler's forte), and the kidney punches of a torpid consumer market ruined by inflation and high interest rates.

As would happen again some 30-odd years later, people throttled back on buying cars—and especially, *Chrysler's* cars.

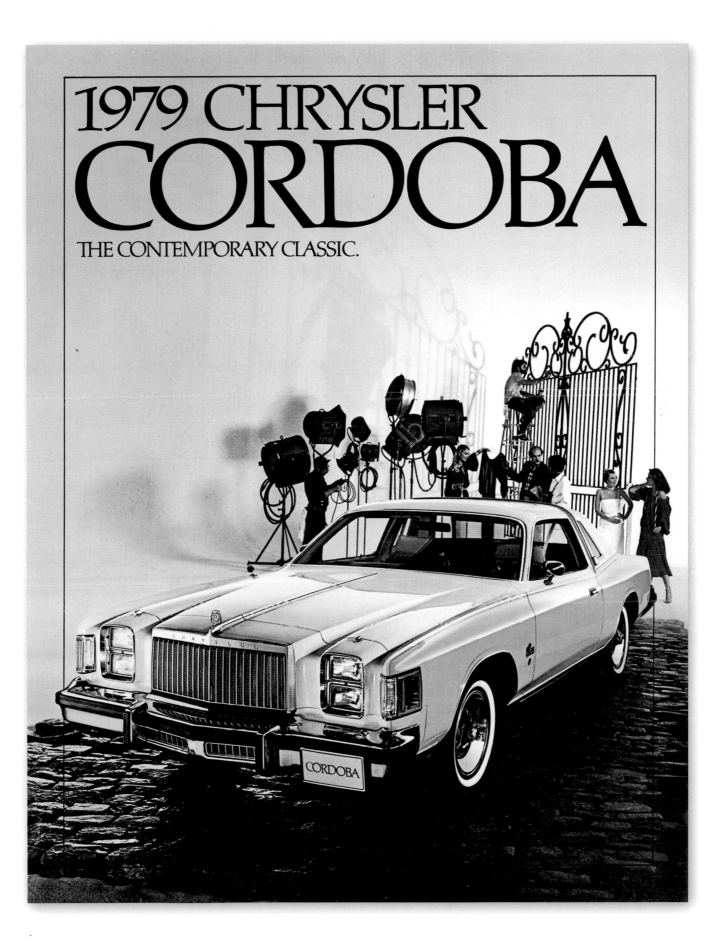

1979 CHRYSLER
CORDOBA

THE CONTEMPORARY CLASSIC.

Cordoba: Things to Know

The '75 Cordoba had a 25.5-gallon fuel tank—comparable in volume to modern full-size SUVs.

Base price (in 1975) was $5,392. Base price in 1983 (the final year) was almost twice that, at $9,580—for one-third less car.

The Cordoba was named after the Spanish city, but its emblem is based on the design of an Argentinian coin.

In 1979 Chrysler dabbled with the idea of a performance-minded Cordoba. This one-year-only version was dubbed "300"—a reference to the late 1950s and early 1960s "letter series" muscle coupes—and came with the same high-performance 360 four-barrel used in the 'Lil Red Express pickup (as well as police interceptor sedans).

An LS version of the 1980–1983 models featured a stylish crosshair grille set in a unique, aero front clip. Nineteen eighty models with the optional 360 V-8 (1980 was the final year for this engine as a Cordoba option) are considered especially collectible.

The 1975 Cordoba was thus a kind of Hail Mary pass—Chrysler's first "small" car, even though by twenty-first-century standards, its 215.3-inch length, 115-inch wheelbase, and 3,975-pound curb weight would easily qualify it as full-size and then some.

Compare the Cordoba's stats against a modern large coupe, such as a 2010 Jaguar XK, which measures just 188.7 inches long and rides on a 108.3-inch wheelbase. Or the 2010 Mercedes SL550, with its Danny DeVito–esque 178.5-inch length and 100.8-inch wheelbase.

A '75 Cordoba was almost two feet longer than a 2010 Toyota Camry Solara, had eight inches more wheelbase, and weighed 900 pounds more. Calling it small was the marketing equivalent of calling waterboarding an enhanced interrogation technique.

The Cordoba was a classy, even stately-looking car that suggested repose rather than rush—from its 15-inch whitewalls to its upright, Rolls-Royce-ish grille with C-H-R-Y-S-L-E-R stamped boldly in relief along the top. A pair of large, round headlights with chrome trim surrounds pointed the way forward. Dashing "Cordoba" script flanked each front fender. A lighted vertical bar adjacent to the Frenched rear quarter windows and optional padded vinyl roof completed the effect.

In the 1970s, personal luxury meant spreadin' out room. And, it meant a Mallomar ride. People in those days didn't expect a luxury barge to corner. They *demanded* that it float along like a coil-sprung BarcaLounger—and at this, the Cordoba excelled, courtesy of its torsion bar front end and semi-elliptical leafs out back that damped the beefy Chrysler's weight as it dipped into potholes and rolled over bumps. Though it had the typically light power steering of the middle 1970s, anti-sway bars at both ends gave the driver good control through the twisties—and this became one of the car's great draws.

Another was—as Ricardo reminded us—an interior that was just as plush as the ride. Cashmere-like knit cloth and vinyl upholstery across comfy bench-style seats was standard. This could be replaced with a velour-stitched 60/40 semibench or, for the True Experience, the famous rich, Corinthian leather. Bucket seats were as *outré* in those days in a luxury car as whitewalls on a Porsche are today. People who wanted sports cars bought sports cars. People who wanted *luxury* bought big boozy cruisermobiles like the Cordoba.

Not that the Cordoba couldn't *run* when it needed to—at least for the first few years of its life.

Not only was a V-8 standard equipment, it was a *big* V-8. The '75 came equipped with a 400-cubic-inch engine with four-barrel carb and single or optional dual exhaust.

The 400 was descended from the old 383—one of the most highly regarded of Chrysler's large V-8s. It was fundamentally the same engine, with a slight overbore and tuned more for torque than all-out horsepower, befitting the times. Even so, the four-barrel version cranked out 235 horsepower—a strong number for 1975. (The same-year Chevy Corvette was down to a 180 horsepower 350 V-8.) The standard transmission was a Torqueflite three-speed automatic with an unusual-for-the-era lock-up converter to boost fuel economy at highway speeds.

Buyers looking to get the most economy out of their Cordoba could select a small-block 318 two-barrel V-8 (150 horsepower) as a credit option. A mid-level 360 four-barrel (180 horsepower) was also available.

A 400, four-barrel-equipped Cordoba delivered easy highway power—as per the TV commercial—and was capable of reaching 60 miles per hour from rest in a leisurely 12 seconds or so.

Despite the desperate times, Cordoba exceeded sales expectations by a considerable margin. First-year production ran to 150,105 units—jumping to 183,146 by 1977.

T-Tops became available—along with standard Autophoritic rust-proofing for the chassis.

In 1978, the front end was restyled—with vertical-stacked square headlights replacing the previous single-rounded units. Many Cordoba aficionados prefer the cleaner and more distinctive look of the first-generation cars—and whether it was the controversial new look or the fact that a *second* energy crunch was hammering big cars, sales began to droop—down almost 60,000 compared with the previous year.

This downturn was the banshee's wail—heralding not just the beginning of the end for Cordoba but also the imminent collapse of Chrysler itself.

By 1979—final year for the "big" Cordoba—sales had dropped to 88,015 units. A desperate downsizing and restyling was attempted for 1980—and though the new car was at least still rear drive and did offer V-8 power, the Cordoba was not long for this world.

The tragic thing is it actually might have worked—except for the fact that Chrysler's quality control had become scandalously sloppy by this time as part of frantic cost-cutting, and buyers justifiably became leery of the Pentastar. Total Cordoba production for 1980 was barely 60,000—and by 1981, even that would look good when Cordoba flat-lined to just under 19,000 sold.

The year 1983 would be the last not just for Cordoba—but for rear-drive and V-8-powered Chrysler coupes for the next 20-plus years.

Want the added sportiness of a classic convertible-style top? Then consider the handsome 1981 Cordoba shown above. It features the Cabriolet Roof Two-Tone Package which includes a Pearl White/Nightwatch Blue paint combination, sailcloth-textured simulated convertible roof and dual chrome remote control mirrors. The Cabriolet Roof Package without two-tone paint is also available on Cordoba and Cordoba LS.

The Cordoba attempted to maintain its luxury image until the end, but by 1983, Chrysler had pinned its hopes for survival on the miserable little front-wheel-drive K cars, and the Cordoba withered on the vine.

COLOSSAL CADDY
COUPE DE VILLE, 1949-1984

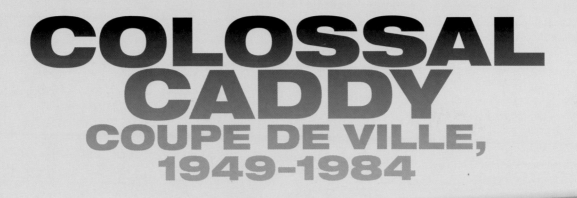

A distinguished Sport Coupe for a Discriminating Clientele

The Coupe de Ville, Cadillac's newest car—a sport model—has been especially designed for those who desire the finest possible automobile combining the smart, low-swept lines of a convertible with the comfort and convenience of a closed car.

Coupe de Ville interiors strike a new note in smart sophistication—always, of course, in the impeccable taste which is traditional with Cadillac. The combination cloth and leather upholstery is severely, yet beautifully tailored. Exposed top bows are in chrome finish. An impression of bright airiness is afforded by exceptionally generous window areas, narrow corner pillars and the newly styled rear window which forms a crescent extending the full width of the rear top area.

Two beautiful interior color combinations are available in the Coupe de Ville—grey-blue cloth with grey leather or coffee-brown cloth with beige leather. Seat backs have leather panels with biscuit type cloth inserts, while the seat cushions are trimmed in cloth. Doors are upholstered in leather with biscuit type cloth inserts. Top interior is in simulated leather.

De Ville means "town" in French. Originally the term was applied to town cars, which were limousines with enclosed cabins for passengers but open-air compartments for the chauffer. Cadillac took liberties with the word when it applied the name *Coupe de Ville* to a high-end, two-door, hardtop version of the Series 62 in 1949.

In Chuck Berry's classic hit song "Maybelline," in which our hero is "motorvatin' over the hill" in his V-8 Ford, he spots Maybelline in a Coupe deVille, the driver of which, apparently, our hero doesn't approve. For whatever reason, our hero pursues the Cadillac, and though his flathead Ford V-8 suffers from the overheating problems endemic in the side-valve design, our hero eventually catches the Cadillac because ". . . nothing outruns my V-8 Ford."

Well, maybe so.

But outrunning Ford-powered hot rods *wasn't* the point when you were behind the wheel of Caddy's ultimate lead sled coupe. If you drove a deVille, you ran from no man. Lesser cars cowed before your presence. Valets took notice. Neighbors were envious.

A Coupe deVille in the driveway was, for nearly 30 years, one of the ultimate American status symbols.

Its doors were longer—and heavier—than the entire front ends of many of today's "large" cars. Made of thick-plate steel that might have made the cut as armor for an M1 Abrams tank, they swung wide on massive hinges bushed with bronze inserts that imparted a deceptive lightness of feel. But watch your fingers! And when one of those mammoth doors got away from you in a parking lot, the consequences for the car parked next to your deVille were painful.

The deVille's expansive hood was a flight deck of shimmering flatness whose far border was marked by the insolent wreath and crest hood ornament.

Inside, this Big Bertha easily swallowed five adults. Wire wheels, whitewalls, chrome, and velour. Phaeton faux convertible top. Seven liters of cast-iron V-8 under the hood. *Eight* liters in the final years of Glory.

What could be better?

The Coupe deVille began life in the late '40s, when it was introduced as a high-trim, pillarless hardtop version of the Series 62 Club Coupe. The 1949 model, the first production example, was powered by a new 160-horsepower 331-cubic-inch OHV V-8 that was more powerful and efficient than the old L-head 346 engine, despite lower displacement. This engine was one of the first of the postwar engines designed to take advantage of the higher octane fuels that were just then becoming available.

The '49 model carried a base price of $3,497—roughly $500 higher than a standard Series 62 Club Coupe.

Interesting touches included a headliner ribbed with chrome trim plates to simulate the appearance of a convertible top. Later versions continued this tradition with vinyl roofs likewise intended to mimic the look of a convertible with its roof up. On early models, the roof was often painted a contrasting color, such as white, to enhance the effect. But unlike the Eldorado, which was available in both coupe and convertible forms for most of its production life, the Coupe deVille was *always* a hardtop coupe, right through to the end.

The new Coupe De Ville was one of the finest and most expensive automobiles in the world in 1949.

Tailfins started off as stylish flips at the rear of the fender; by the late 1950s, they'd grown to cartoonish proportions. It would get worse before it got better.

Though expensive, a Coupe deVille was more accessible than the outrageously priced Eldorado, yet it offered virtually the same hulking curb appeal—and with better body integrity than the leak-prone Eldo ragtop. As a result, it was produced in fairly large numbers, even early on—and eventually, would become one of Cadillac's biggest sellers.

Second-year production—4,507 units—was more than *twice* the '49 run of 2,150 and *eight* times more than the 523 car first-year run of the Eldorado, which appeared four years later, in early 1953.

By 1956 (last year of the first generation) Cadillac was selling more than 24,000 Coupe deVilles annually—versus the *combined* Eldorado production (Seville hardtop *and* Biarritz convertible) of 6,050 cars that year.

Internally, the Coupe deVille was looked upon as Cadillac's money maker—a prestige car that was also profitable. It was the model that made the lower-volume, more-expensive-to-build Eldorado possible—and it did it without cheapening the Caddy mystique.

Nineteen fifty-seven marked the appearance of the second-generation Coupe deVille, notable not just for its jet-age, wide-bodied styling but also for its potent new 365-cubic-inch V-8, which broke the 300-horsepower barrier (in the Coupe deVille) for the first time—and for the addition of 3 more inches of wheelbase, now up to 129 inches from the previous year's 126. Overall length remained the same at 200.5 inches. Weight stood at an impressive 4,620 pounds—bulkiness surpassed only by the 4,930-pound Eldorado Biarritz convertible.

Two years later, the deVille (like the Eldorado before it) became a distinct model line in its own right and no longer a high-end Series 62. The car was a *spectacle*: 225 inches long and 4,700 pounds, its stern capped off with massive pillars of steel intended perhaps to function as air rudders, the means by which the dreadnought could be steered through the ether. In fact the car was maneuvered via ultra-low-effort power steering enhanced by the mechanical leverage of a hula hoop–sized steering wheel. Course changes could be effected by finger-dialing to the left or right, as needed.

Under the hood, a new 325-horsepower 390 stood ready; in 1964 displacement increased to 429 cubes—with horsepower pegged at 340.

The year 1965 marked a stylistic U-turn for Cadillac (and General Motors). The influence of Harley Earl, who had retired a few years previously, was waning. The new ethic, as defined by his protégé and successor, Bill Mitchell, blossomed fully with the introduction of the fifth-generation Coupe deVille.

Voluptuous curves and baroque forms gave way to sharp angles and a more serious demeanor. The previous wraparound front glass was retired in favor of a smaller, flatter windshield, which fed into a squared-off roof that cut sharply back toward the trunk. Fins, were no more. The slab-sided rear quarters now pinched upward, ending in fully integrated vertical taillight buckets that would remain a Cadillac styling element

THE NEW STANDARD OF THE WORLD IN ELEGANCE!

Coupe de Ville

The completely new profile and interior elegance of the Coupe de Ville assure its continued affection in the hearts of the world's motorists. Inspect it from any viewpoint, and you will discover a rare discernment and imagination by its designers . . . craftsmanship and quality by its builders. Magnificent interior fabrics include Camden cloth in hues of gray, blue and fawn with matching leathers . . . silver-black Coronado with white leather . . . green Coronado with green metallic leather . . . turquoise-black Coronado with turquoise metallic leather . . . and rose Coronado with rose metallic leather.

Today Cadillac is working to rebuild its image in its home market and is barely a footnote in the rest of the world, but in the 1950s the GM division set the world's standard for motoring elegance.

Left: **For the first 10 years** of its existence, the Coupe de Ville was just a luxury trim package for the Series 62 coupe. Beginning in 1959, it became its own distinct model.

Volkswagen drivers who saw this sight in their rearview mirrors were well advised to get out of the way.

through the 1980s. Vertically stacked quad headlights and a wider egg-crate grille up front completed the ensemble.

Base price was up to $5,419, but sales stayed very strong nonetheless, with 43,345 sold that year—representing a substantial uptick over the previous year. Sales continued upward bound through 1966 (50,580), 1967 (52,905), 1968 (63,935), 1969 (65,755), and into 1970, when an impressive 76,043 Coupe deVilles went home with their new owners.

The 1971 restyle—which lasted through the '76 model run—represents the apotheosis of Coupe deVille enormousness. Wheelbase grew to its ultimate expression, 130 inches, while overall length now extended nearly 231 inches from stem to stern (in 1972). A

5,000-pound curb weight was achieved the moment the driver sat down. With two aboard, a sixth-generation Coupe deVille was easily a 5,200-pound weighty waddler.

To get it all going, Caddy plopped in a 500-cubic-inch V-8, shared with the Eldorado but detuned slightly to 375 horsepower (versus 400). The 1970 500 cuber would also be the most powerful of the series—but unfortunately, not for long. In 1971, the rated output of this engine declined to 345 horsepower (365 in the top-of-the-line Eldorado) and the trend would grow worse in the ensuing years, as GM struggled to make V-8s built for an era of Who Cares gas mileage and indifference to exhaust emissions compliance with the EPA-regulated and OPEC-strangled '70s.

The mid-1960s Cadillac Coupe de Ville is arguably the cleanest, most elegant automobile that was ever designed during Bill Mitchell's tenure as head of GM design. It was also, perhaps less arguably, the finest automobile ever built in America.

Below: **Imagine a two-door coupe** that is 230 inches long. That's over 19 feet. For a two-door. You can't help but admire that kind of wretched excess. In 1973, Cadillac finally abandoned the hardtop configuration that had defined the Coupe de Ville since its debut in order to meet rollover standards that the government abandoned before they were ever implemented.

THE DeVILLE SERIES

The Coupe de Ville
AMERICA'S FAVORITE LUXURY CAR.

The 1976 Cadillac Coupe deVille is again out front with all the important considerations Americans seem to want most in their luxury cars. That is . . . elegant lines, traditional styling and full-sized responsiveness. What's the secret behind DeVille's popularity? Consistently high resale value, for one thing. For another, standard features that range from Automatic Climate Control to Power Door Locks. And it's the features you can specify . . . like Cadillac's Electronic-Fuel-Injected Engine, Astroroof and an AM/FM Signal-Seeking Stereo Radio with a 24-hour weather band.

By 1975, the eight-liter 500-cubic-inch V-8 was making a desperately sad 190 horsepower, less than half its rated 1970 output. But despite this underhood emasculation, the public still revered Caddy's vehicular blunderbuss, perhaps understanding that they would be the last of their kind.

The year 1973, as it turned out, would be the year for six-figure sales—112,849—a trend that actually lasted all the way through 1979, when 121,890 were sold. This in spite of the slight downsizing/restyle that took place in 1977, when the Coupe deVille lost seven inches of wheelbase and about nine inches of overall length. The 500 was gone now, too. A new 425 was as big as it got—and even that would not last long.

Soon, deVille had to make do with 368 cubes and a rather wretched 150 net horsepower.

Sales began to free-fall soon thereafter, perhaps in recognition that the good times were coming to a close. The 1980 model year saw a total of 55,490 sold—less than half the 1979 run of 121,890.

Two years later, in 1984, the Last of the Large left the shipyards—propelled by a completely sad 105-horsepower diesel V-8 hashed together in haste from an Oldsmobile-built gasoline V-8. It was either that or the even more problematic variable displacement V-8-6-4 that, in theory, operated on four or six cylinders under light loads to conserve fuel but in actual practice was one of GM's greatest fiascos of the century and cost the automaker dearly with consumers.

Coupe de Ville: Things to Know

Cadillac's signature tail fins were reportedly inspired by the World War II–era P-38 Lightning fighter.

The pillarless coupe design of the first-generation Coupe deVille was intended to provide the airy, open feel of a convertible with the body integrity/solidity of an enclosed coupe.

A deVille convertible was offered during the mid- to late 1960s; however, it was not a Coupe deVille.

Though it began life as one of Cadillac's top models, by the '77 model year the Coupe deVille had become Cadillac's entry-level car, replacing the discontinued Calais in this role. It carried a base price of $9,810.

A Phaeton Package offered in the mid-'70s was intended to duplicate the convertible look—similar to the chrome interior bows used in the first-generation cars.

The door slammed shut for good in 1985, when a Camry-sized front-wheel-drive pretender to the laurels appeared. Cadillac would continue trying to pawn off these downscaled deVilles on an unwilling public through 1993, when the much-abused designation was finally allowed to rest in peace.

From a collectibility standpoint, deVilles—especially '76 and older models—are very desirable. These barges are even more impressive today than they were back in the day—because the disparity between their outsized proportions and the run-of-the-mill full-size car of the modern era is so striking. Early models through about 1976 with the 500-cube V-8 are more collectible—and command higher prices. But the 1977–1984 models are almost as entertaining to operate, nearly as visually impressive—and much more affordable. They're also much more *available*, having been produced in very large numbers and (for the most part) having been owned by older drivers who tended to baby them.

Cadillac shrunk most of its models in 1977, but the rear-wheel Coupe de Ville was still a large car by any standard.

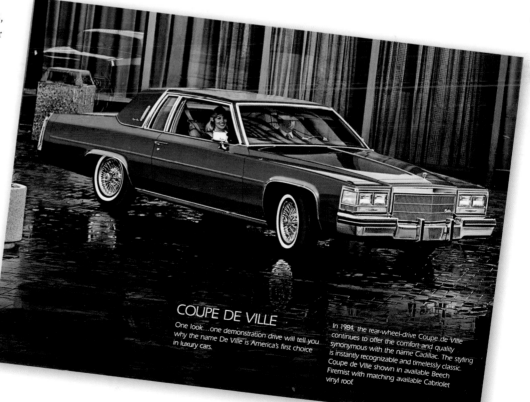

COUPE DE VILLE

One look...one demonstration drive will tell you why the name De Ville is America's first choice in luxury cars.

In 1984, the rear-wheel-drive Coupe de Ville continues to offer the comfort and quality synonymous with the name Cadillac. The styling is instantly recognizable and timelessly classic. Coupe de Ville shown in available Beech Firemist with matching available Cabriolet vinyl roof.

BUSTY BUICK RIVIERA COUPE
1963-1985

The understated, uncluttered look of the modern, fashionably dressed woman is similarly expressed in the body-tailored, classic elegance of the Riviera. Uninterrupted by needless strips of chrome beading, its sophisticated custom-coachwork appearance is the result of an exclusive new body construction technique. Like the finest custom imports, the Riviera's sheer glass side windows have no metal frames. The unique, sleek Riviera look is enhanced by its windscreen and rear window being sealed tight to the body . . . instead of being encased in more ordinary metal and rubber frames. Quality is apparent everywhere. Approaching the Riviera from any direction, the appreciative woman will be eye-delighted by its exceptionally clean, sculptured lines, the predominant characteristic of its trend-setting styling.

To Her...the Riviera offers magnificence...inside and out

With its new-for-1963 Riviera, Buick created a new genre of automobile: the personal luxury coupe.

At the dawn of the second century of the automobile, GM's Buick division had been outsourced (and downsized) to China, where the brand is hugely popular. On its home turf, however, Buick had become synonymous with senior citizen discounts and airport rental car fleets.

It is quite something to contemplate the decline of one of America's most desirable brands of cars into one of its most forgettable—all in the space of about 30 years.

And nothing will give you a sense of what has been lost more than a look back at one of Buick's greatest hits ever, the sheetmetal Jayne Mansfield of its time—the seductive Riviera coupe.

Non-Buick people may not know it, but the Riviera nameplate goes back many years before the introduction of the now-famous '63 coupe. Buick used it to designate the pillarless hardtop coupes and sedans that appeared in the late 1940s and continued through the early to mid-1950s.

A man will appreciate the fact that the best Buick engine . . . the premium-performance 325-horsepower Wildcat V-8 . . . powers the Riviera. (A larger 340-horsepower Wildcat is available at extra cost to those men who are *super*-performance-minded!) As finely balanced as a competition engine, this precision-crafted Buick power plant provides the snap and sparkle that's equally (and stupendously) competent on turnpike or boulevard. It's teamed with Buick's super-smooth Turbine Drive (standard equipment). And to keep its sparkling engine from choking up or going flat, the Riviera has dual exhausts as standard equipment . . . and a totally efficient, long-lasting muffler.

To Him...the Riviera delivers perfectly powered performance

For more personal enjoyment... Riviera...by Buick

Buick marketed the style and luxury of its new Riviera to female buyers. For male buyers, the division touted the strong performance of the car's optional 425-cubic-inch V-8 engine.

A not-so-subtle subtext in the advertising for Buick's Riviera: if you buy this elegant, luxurious car, you might end up in the back seat with a hottie like this.

What would Spock drive if they took away the keys to the Enterprise? Why, a Riv, of course.

The '63 coupe, however, was something entirely new.

It made its production debut in late 1962 and was intended to do two things: First, help Buick rebuild after the recessionary slump of the late '50s, during which overall sales had declined significantly; second, to give Buick something to lure potential buyers away from Ford and its successful Thunderbird franchise.

It was an absolutely striking car—and also a very different car. Where the Thunderbird was classically styled and almost baroque, the Riviera was daringly modern, with a knife-edge styling defined by sharp pleats and angles. The entire works was muscular and coiled—a sheetmetal hit man for young executives on their way up.

And it was priced that way, too. With a few options, a '63 Riviera could cost $5,000 or even more—a tidy sum for a personal car at a time when a typical family car sold for around $3,000 well equipped.

Standard under the hood was Buick's nailhead V-8, displacing 401 cubic inches, and the two-ton Riv needed every inch of displacement.

But for such a gigantic machine, the Riv handled and stopped fairly well.

The '63 model featured standard power steering and high-performance (for the day) power-boosted aluminum-finned drum brakes all around.

Inside were low-backed bucket seats, which could be upholstered in vinyl, cloth, or leather. This was a full-on luxury coupe, so even cruise control was on the options list. Though common in the modern era, back in the early 1960s, cruise control was a feature usually found on higher-end cars only. (Technical aside: The Riv's system was a vacuum-mechanical system, unlike today's electronically controlled systems.)

A significant technological update appeared in time for the '64 model year, when GM's new three-speed Turbo-Hydramatic automatic transmission entered production. This was a major improvement over the old two-speed units (High and Low forward gearing) used previously. Buick marketed this transmission as the Super Turbine 400. (GM would later market it across its divisions as the THM400.)

Another upgrade came under the hood, with the addition of a bigger, stronger 425 V-8. This mega-motor was rated at a very stout 340 horsepower in single four-barrel form. But buyers could step it up by ordering the optional dual-carb Super Wildcat version, which bumped the output to 360 horsepower.

As the muscle car era entered full flower, Buick decided to bulk up the Riv even further with a Gran Sport package that included the Super Wildcat 425 V-8, dual exhausts, and aggressive 3.42 axle ratio.

This was a roller that could definitely roll.

Road testers clocked examples equipped with the optional 425 V-8 as being capable of reaching 60 miles per hour in under eight seconds through the twin turbine automatic transmission—with a top speed close to 130 miles per hour. For comparison, this performance is comparable to an early 1980s Ford Mustang GT 5.0 liter.

Buick introduced the second-generation Riv in 1966. Unlike the original, the '66-up Riviera shared a platform with another GM car—*two* of them, actually. The Oldsmobile Toronado and the Cadillac Eldorado. However, it did not share the front-wheel-drive layout of its sister cars. The Riviera also retained its own unique, Buick-specific drivetrain.

The 425 Wildcat remained at the heart of things for 1966, but by 1967 was retired in favor of an updated version of the Buick V-8, punched out to 430 cubes. In 1970 Buick released the 455-cubic-inch version of its biggest V-8. This engine was one of the

For 1970, Buick made its largest, most powerful engine available on the Riviera. The 455-cubic-inch mill cranked out 370 horsepower and over 500 lbs-ft of torque.

When you change a classic automobile, you'd better change it for the better.
We did.
The 1970 Riviera. Long, flowing hood. Trim rear deck. The look of the original personal car. Much the same…only, as we said, better.
There's a new grille and front bumper ensemble that looks like a product of the sculptor's chisel.
The 1970 Riviera profile. Clean. Flowing. Unbroken. Classic.
The new Riviera powerplant. 455 cubic inches. 370 horsepower. Smooth. Responsive. It's the biggest, the most reliable engine ever made by Buick.

Riviera standard equipment. Just what you might expect…just about everything.
Then there's AccuDrive, Buick's advance design suspension system. AccuDrive affords an unheard of degree of handling ease and control.
So your Riviera drives like it looks…beautifully.
And Riviera quality, superb quality. It's the kind of quality and dependability that's built right into every Riviera, and every Buick.
Quality. Style. Performance. They're the things you expect in a truly classic automobile.
Just as you expected, they're present in generous measure in the 1970 Riviera.

1970 BUICK RIVIERA.
SOMETHING TO BELIEVE IN.

Riviera.

Some of the equipment shown is available at extra cost.

Riviera GS.

Inside the Riviera
Discover new. Get inside: sit down; sink in. Relaxation is yours. The 1971 Riviera. A unique experience in unmatched comfort. Totally new dimensions in driving pleasure. Front head room: 37.7 inches; Front leg room: 42.7 inches; Rear leg room: 35.6 inches; Front shoulder room: 64.3 inches; Rear shoulder room: 59.3 inches. (Note: Riviera interior and exterior dimensions are approximations in inches.)

Outside the Riviera
Aerodynamic styling. Longer. Wider. Daring new design. The 1971 Riviera is motion-sculptured giving an image of movement even when standing still. In a word: excitement. Length: 217.4 inches; Width: 79.9 inches; Height: 54.0 inches; Wheelbase: 122.0 inches.

Riviera Performance
Something to believe in. Unexcelled craftsmanship. Engineering excellence.

Standard engine: 455-4 V8; Compression Ratio: 8.5:1; Displacement: 455 C.I.D.; Carburetion: 4-barrel.

Transmission: 3-speed Turbo Hydra-matic 400 automatic transmission.

Rear Axle Ratio: Riviera: 2.93; Riviera GS: 3.42 with positive traction. Please consult your Buick dealer on available ratios.

Riviera Comfort
Luxurious. Convenient. Features you'd expect to find only in Riviera.

Yours to enjoy: New Full-Flo ventilation system; heater and defroster; recessed windshield wiper blades; new full-foam contoured seats; semi-suspended accelerator pedal for more comfortable operation; deep pile carpeting, front and rear; front door-operated interior light; electric clock; inside trunk light; smoking set; front and rear ash trays; new, more convenient seat belt assembly; cushioned head restraints; luxurious new interior appointments; newly designed instrument cluster for easier reading and serviceability; increased visibility, front and rear; inside hood lock release; increased trunk capacity; outside rear view mirror; arm rests; front folding seat back latches; anti-theft key warning buzzer; anti-theft steering column lock, plus many more comfort and convenience features your Buick dealer will be pleased to discuss with you.

Riviera Special Features
Features to make your motoring more pleasurable: Buick's AccuDrive with forward mounted steering gear and linkage; 3-speed Turbo Hydra-matic 400 Automatic Transmission; variable ratio power steering; self-adjusting power front disc brakes with composite cast iron rear drum brakes; dual exhausts with stainless steel wrapped mufflers; Full-Flow oil filter; semi-closed cooling system; 6,000 mile lubricated front suspension; Delcotron generator with integral voltage regulator; rear view mirror mounted on inside of windshield; time-modulated carburetor choke control; side guard beam construction for added protection; new evaporative emission control system; four jet windshield washers.

The available Riviera Gran Sport
A high performance 455-4 V8 engine that runs on low lead gas. Includes a specially calibrated 3-speed Turbo Hydra-matic 400 Automatic Transmission. Heavy-duty suspension. Positive traction differential (3.42 axle ratio standard). "Riviera GS" monogram on front fender. H78 x 15 bias-belted white wall tires are standard.

Some of the equipment shown is available at extra cost. For information on MaxTrac, Buick's exclusive traction control system, please refer to Page 5.

Riviera.

3

elegance and romance.

Above: **The year 1971** marked the beginning of the Dark Ages of American performance cars. Automakers began lowering compression ratios in preparation for the coming of unleaded gasoline, which was mandated for the 1975 model-year cars. As a result, the output of the standard Riviera's 455-cubic-inch engine fell to 255 horsepower, though a Gran Sport version offered an additional 10 horsepower.

The downsized 1977 Riviera was, in essence, a restyled LeSabre coupe. Buick dropped the 455 engine after 1976, leaving the 350 V-8 as its largest offering. Since this was too small and underpowered to motivate the 5,000-pound Riviera, Buick borrowed a 403-cubic-inch V-8 from sister division Oldsmobile.

most impressive American V-8s ever built, then or since. Its 360 horsepower wasn't what made it exceptional, however. At the time, many others were offering about the same (or more). Rather, what made the Buick 455 so tremendously formidable was its 450-plus foot pounds of torque—with the peak twist happening at just off fast idle. This made it the equal of top-dog muscle car motors—including the legendary Chrysler 426 street Hemi—when it came to street performance.

In the smaller, lighter GSX (corporate cousin of the Chevy Chevelle and Pontiac GTO), this same basic engine could deliver high 12-second quarter-mile time slips through an automatic transmission and with the AC running. The six-passenger Riviera with Strato-bench seats wasn't quite as quick, perhaps, but you still messed with it at your own risk.

As the calendar rolled over into the '70s, GM unveiled a completely new, third-gen Riv that was every bit as striking as the original '63 model—and which earned its place in the pantheon of automotive greats.

The boat-tail 1971–1973—with its big-hipped, pontoon-style rear fenders, sloping rear canopy glass, and seemingly endless flight deck of a hood up front—looked like absolutely nothing else on the road. Contrast-color vinyl roofs provided the finishing touch.

Buick's Jerry Hirschberg is given credit for the boat-tail cars and was inspired by an earlier concept penned by GM's legendary Bill Mitchell.

These third-gen cars remain one of GM's most iconic and instantly recognizable designs. General Manager Lee Mays described it as a "triumph of automotive styling," though he himself reportedly did not care for the look.

It was also an enormous car—stretching a *Lusitania*-like 223.4 inches by 1973 (and this was a *two-door coupe*) and riding on a 122-inch wheelbase and weighing close to 5,000 pounds fully fueled and with driver onboard.

Though it had become a true land yacht in terms of size as well as luxury amenities, Buick still offered performance equipment—including a Stage 1 package that centered on the 455 V-8 (now rated at 330 horsepower), firm-shift THM400 automatic, positraction rear, chrome engine dress-up kit, plus a new firm-ride suspension based on the then-new radial tire. In fact, the '71 Riv got a unique radial tire designed just for it—designed to work with the car's Accudrive front suspension geometry, which worked to limit body lean under hard cornering.

Acceleration was impressive: 0–60 in just over 8 seconds with mid-high 15-second quarter-mile capability.

In 1974 came a new look that was more subdued. Though the Riv was still a king of the road in terms of its bulk, it had lost much of its previously distinctive styling—as well as power.

The boat-tail treatment was replaced with more conventional sheet metal; quad headlights up front were similar to what you'd see on other GM cars that year—a clear sign of the trend toward badge-engineered cars that, in later years, would cause GM's share of the U.S. auto market to slip from a 50-plus percent in 1970 to less than 24 percent by 2009. The 455 was still in the lineup, in name at least—but its sails had been

The Riviera abandoned rear-wheel drive for the 1979 model year and succumbed to the trend toward front-wheel drive. The front-wheel-drive version of the car was moderately successful, selling 50,000 to 60,000 units per year.

Riviera T Type.

Riviera Convertible.

Riviera Coupe interior.

The Riviera Coupe combines the classic elegance of traditional Riviera styling with fully independent suspension, front-wheel drive and a standard 5.0 litre V-8. The Riviera T Type is equipped with the enthusiast in mind: 3.8 litre turbocharged V-6 engine with SFI and Gran Touring suspension. The Riviera Convertible adds all the singular experience of top-down motoring to all the luxury, comfort and elegance that is so much a part of every Riviera. Seating areas are upholstered in fine cloth, or, if you wish, leather and vinyl or leather and vinyl with suede. There is luxurious cut-pile carpeting, and the look of rich woodgrain enhances the instrument panel and doors.

Riviera Coupe.

In 1982, Buick introduced the convertible version of the Riviera. This was the first time that Buick offered a topless Riv in the model's 20-year history.

trimmed considerably. The final year (1976) saw it detuned to 230–245 horsepower. This was still decent for the time, however—and though the 1974–1976 Riv may not have been as visually glorious as its predecessors, it was still a large-living hunka hunka burning love.

Smart shoppers bought them while they still could.

Beginning in 1977, GM steadily downsized (and de-powered) the Riv. The 455 got dropped (replaced by the smaller 350 and Oldsmobile-sourced 403) and the car's wheelbase was trimmed to 115.9 inches. These would be the last of the rear-drive Rivs as Buick (and GM) began the shift over to front-drive and (in time) compact-size versions of what had once been America's heaviest hitters.

Nineteen seventy-three was the last year before four-wheel drive.

The last physically substantial Rivieras were built between 1979 and 1985. These cars were slightly larger than the Regal coupe of the same era—and still offered a high level of luxury, although not much in the way of gumption to go with it. Three hundred and fifty cubes was as big as it got, with many examples leaving the factory with the smaller, Olds-sourced 307 or Buick's 231 V-6. This was also the first time a Riviera offered less than a V-8, though in its defense, the little six was available turbocharged. Briefly—and tragically—an Oldsmobile-sourced diesel V-8 was also available.

By 1986, the classic Riviera shell itself was no more—replaced by a downscaled runt of a car that was smaller than a mid-'70s Chevy Nova. It was also crippled by not-ready-for-prime-time technology, such as a digital interface that caused endless problems for owners, dealers, and GM's warranty department.

A last gasp was attempted in 1995, but the Koi-faced, pinched-butt thing that Buick created never resonated with buyers. In 1999, the final year, fewer than 2,000 were made.

Of all Rivieras, the first-generation and early '70s boat-tail models are without question the most interesting and collectible. Prices on the first-generation cars are fairly high, but the quirky 1971–1973s remain very accessible. They're also big fun to own, just as they were when new.

Riviera: Things to Know

Sales of the first-generation Riviera, approximately 112,244 from 1963 to 1965, easily exceeded the total number of cars produced during the final four years of Riviera production, from 1995 to 1999, when approximately 91,914 were made.

Early boat-tail Rivieras had a louvered trunk that was part of the car's ventilation system. Leakage problems (rain water as well as engine exhaust) forced a redesign, so only the '71 cars have this feature.

Buick offered an early form of traction control (Max Trac) on the 1971–1973 boat-tail Riviera that limited wheelspin when the drive wheels encountered a slick surface by cutting back engine power.

The Riviera, over its lifetime, offered V-8s, V-6s, turbochargers, superchargers, and multiple carburetors.

The Riviera remained in continuous production for 36 years, making it one of GM's longest-lived most successful models.

The Riv soldiered on into the 1990s, but the front drivers, while nice enough cars, weren't the sorts of vehicles that would capture the imagination of Vulcans like Spock.

ALOSAURUS
AMC
MATADOR 1971-1978

The Matador is the new American Motors car designed to make the other intermediate cars look stingy. It has more room for you and your family than any other car in its class.

To make the ride even more comfortable, we built it on a longer wheelbase than you get with Ford's Torino, Plymouth's Satellite or Chevrolet's Chevelle.

And it's priced to compete with them all, despite the fact there's no such thing as a stripped model in the line.

Matador hardtop in Matador Red with vinyl top.

AMC's Matador began life as a replacement for the company's Rambler Rebel, though *replacement* is a strong word, since the Matador was, for all practical purposes, a Rebel with more masculine styling cues.

By the mid-1970s, American automakers were under the gun to reduce both the size and the fuel consumption of their offerings. Gas shortages, price spikes—and the growing presence of Japanese competition—were having the same effect on Detroit's lead sleds that the Chixilub asteroid impact had on dinosaurs some 60 million years ago.

Still, traditional American rollers weren't going down without a fight. AMC may have been forced by circumstances to drop the Ambassador after the 1974 run, but it still had a plus-size contender in the Matador.

The Matador first appeared in 1971 and by the '75 model year officially succeeded the Ambassador as AMC's big car—and would carry the flag through 1978. Police variants survived in fleets into the '80s—on the strength of their huge-for-the-times 401-cubic-inch V-8s with more than 200 horsepower and 130 miles per hour top-speed capability.

Most people remember the coupe more so than the sedan. It—unlike the Ambassador coupe—rode on its own, modified and shortened 114-inch wheelbase.

By 1974, it had become a separate model in its own right.

Styling was typically AMC unusual, with bulbous, almost amphibian-like headlights and wavy-gravy side sculpting. Huge rear quarter glass and an expansive front windshield did provide excellent visibility.

No convertible was ever offered by the factory, but you could opt for a very groovy vinyl-covered landau roof.

AMC offered two unusual variants in the mid-1970s: the Oleg Cassini and Barcelona editions. The first was named after one of Jackie O's favorite *haute couture* stylists and came painted tuxedo black, copper, or white with matching landau roof.

These models had their own special interiors with deep pile copper carpeting and copper buttons on the seat upholstery. Oleg Cassini's signature graced the glove box and trunk lid—and Cassini himself helped promo the car in AMC advertising.

The Oleg Cassini edition was available for just two model years, from 1974 through 1975.

In 1976, the Matador Barcelona edition appeared. Like the Oleg Cassini edition, it was designed as a response to the Chrysler Cordoba, Pontiac Grand Prix, Buick Riviera, and other large personal luxury coupes of the time. It was even more over-the-top than the Cassini edition and featured two-tone Ginger Metallic and Sand Tan (1976) or Autumn Red Metallic and Claret Metallic (1977–1978) paint with crushed velvet upholstery inside.

AMC also upgraded the handling attributes of the car with front *and* rear anti-sway bars, plus large-for-the-era GR78x15 radials on unique slotted mag wheels.

In 1978, buyers could order the Barcelona package on Matador sedans, too.

Wagons, meanwhile, had their own slew of special features—including a rear-facing third-row bench seat (a feature that today's *safety-uber-alles* culture wouldn't tolerate).

Matador powerplant choices initially ranged from an economical inline six (either 232 or 258cubic inches and 135 or 150 horsepower, respectively) to three available V-8s. In 1971, buyers could pick a 304 V-8 (210 horsepower) or 360 V-8 in either 245 or 285-horsepower tune.

It's not well known, but a high-performance Matador Machine was available—though just briefly.

Machine coupes—of which fewer than 50 were made—featured hopped-up versions of the 360 and (later) 401 V-8s, with dual exhaust—as well as a heavy-duty suspension package and trim upgrades. Unlike the Rebel Machine, however, the wild red, white, and blue paint and decal package wasn't used.

Everyone, even the folks running AMC, agreed that the original Matador coupe styling was uninspired, at best, so the company introduced a much more contemporary-looking fastback coupe design for the 1974 model year.

AMC ▲ MATADOR

Matador Brougham Coupe with optional "Oleg Cassini" Package in P1 Classic Black with black vinyl roof.

Matador X in H8 Autumn Red Metallic.

The stylish new Matador fastback coupe made quite an impression, earning a styling award from *Car and Driver* magazine as well as an appearance in the 1974 James Bond film *The Man with the Golden Gun*.

These cars were capable of 8-second 0–60 runs and ate up the quarter-mile in 16 seconds flat.

In 1972, the formerly Ambassador (and Machine) exclusive 401 became available across the Matador line, but was now rated at 225 horsepower. However, the power drop was at least partially on paper only—and was in large part due to the new way horsepower was rated and advertised.

Previously, automakers had been permitted to tout an engine's output as measured on a stand, with no power-sapping accessories or exhaust—and often, with a tune job that did not reflect what an actual production engine, as installed in the car, delivered. The new SAE *net* horsepower ratings gave a more realistic measure of an engine's output. Still, there was some actual power loss, as AMC, like everyone else, dialed back on compression ratios and camshaft profiles to comply with getting-stricter federal emissions requirements and the public's desire for more efficient vehicles.

To its enduring credit, AMC bucked the general trend toward less and less powerful engines—at least for a while. In 1973, the output of the Matador's optional 401 climbed to 255 horsepower, which for comparison was 5 horsepower stronger than Pontiac's standard 455 V-8 and the Chevy 454 big-block that powered the Corvette. The Matador's 360 V-8 also jumped to 195–220 horsepower versus 175–195 horsepower the previous year. These were among the strongest factory-spec engines available in an American car that year.

While the 360 got dialed back again in 1974 (to the same 175–195 horsepower as in 1972), the 401 stayed strong with the same 255 horsepower rating as before. Unfortunately, the appearance of catalytic converters in 1975 resulted in the disappearance of the 401. That year, the 175-horsepower 360 became the Matador's strongest available engine. Most left the factory with the much more meager 110-horsepower 258-cube inline six or the step-up 150-horsepower 304 V-8.

Dual exhausts were also history at AMC—and everywhere else.

Despite this, AMC found plenty of willing Matador buyers. In 1975, some 49,890 were sold. Add wagons and sedans to the mix, and total production for 1975 rises to more than 60,000 units.

By 1977, however, the Matador was beginning to feel the pinch. Its 360 V-8 had been emasculated to a rather desperate 129 horsepower, which in a nearly two-ton coupe resulted in equally desperate acceleration. AMC was trying to keep the Matador in tune with the times, but big cars must have big engines and the enfeebled 360 was simply no longer up to the job.

Nineteen seventy-eight would be its final year.

Though horsepower got bumped a bit to 140 (for the top-of-the-line 360), buyers had lost interest in the unusually styled—and now underpowered—Matador. Only about 6,800 coupes and sedans were made that year. Wagons did better, with 3,746 of them finding homes.

Collectors have focused more on the sportier, smaller AMX and Javelin, but one can acquire a perfect or near-perfect Matador for a fraction of the cost. Score one of the unusual and rare-to-find-today Oleg Cassini or Barcelona versions and you're all but guaranteed to be the only person in your county (maybe your state) who owns one.

individual reclining seats in velveteen crush fabric are only a few. You'll also find such desirable trim items as wheel covers, 12" day/night mirror, dual horns and electric clock. Protection features include an inside hood release, sturdy front and rear bumper guards. All standard at Matador's moderate price.

The Barcelona package adds even more luxury. Special two-tone paint, Landau vinyl roof with opera windows and a host of comfort, convenience and appearance features make the Matador Barcelona a mid-size value with outstanding appeal.

Take a look at the Matador Coupe and you'll be impressed. Take a ride and you'll be convinced that no other car in Matador's class offers so much for a comparable price.

Matador: with features that make it an extraordinary value. And, backed by the exclusive BUYER PROTECTION PLAN.

Matador 2-dr. Coupe

AMC MATADOR COUPE

If you're impressed by big car comfort and sleek automotive styling in a mid-sized car, you'll marvel at the Matador Coupe. In Matador, you travel in luxury with smooth, quiet riding qualities over all kinds of roads.

The 1978 Matador features an extensive variety of luxury equipment as standard. Power steering, power front disc brakes, automatic transmission and

Matador Barcelona 2-door Coupe

26

AMC took the Matador coupe's reputation for high style and ran with it, producing a number of special editions, such as the Oleg Cassini edition, developed with input from the American fashion designer of the same name, and the Barcelona II coupe, which featured a padded Landau roof and opera windows.

The Matador coupe got off to a strong sales start, selling over 62,000 units for the 1974 model year, but by 1978, the final year of production, the bloom was off the rose and sales fell to 2,000 units.

Matador: Things to Know

The 401-powered Matador police car was capable of reaching 60 miles per hour in about seven seconds and had a top speed of nearly 130 miles per hour—making it one of the quickest and fastest police vehicles of the 1970s.

The '74 Matador coupe won *Car and Driver*'s Best Styled Car Award that year.

A Matador had a starring role in the James Bond movie *The Man with the Golden Gun*.

Matador Machines are extremely rare, with no more than two or three thought to still be in existence.

AMC's advertising slogan in the early '70s came in the form of a question: "What's a Matador?"

CHUNKY CHEVY
MONTE CARLO COUPE
1970-1988

This is Monte Carlo by Chevrolet.

There is a species of American land shark that once prowled the highways and byways of the United States in great fleets, but which have become as extinct as Megalodon—the 60-foot ancestor of today's Great Whites: the oversize personal luxury coupe.

Rusting hulks in weedy fields are the silent monuments of their passing.

One of these masters of metal was Chevy's Monte Carlo—named after the country, the race, or the literary character—as you prefer.

Like its sister cars, the Pontiac Grand Prix and Oldsmobile Cutlass, the Monte Carlo was based on GM's G-body full-size coupe platform. Unlike its sisters, the Monte was not a child of the '60s (first year was 1970) and would never be built as anything but a hardtop coupe.

Chevy General Manager Pete Estes is credited with conceiving the Monte; Dave Holls for sculpting the look—which was defined by a massive prow (the result of extending the frame by some two inches from the cowl forward) flanked by broad, semipontooned fenders. Formal rear quarter windows and a pompadour semifastback roofline completed the shell. Each end was punctuated by chromed steel slabs hung low and wide. A set of single headlights gave the '70 an alert and hungry look—and clearly differentiated it from the quad-headlighted Chevelle and Caprice coupes.

When he had headed Pontiac division, John Z. DeLorean had championed the idea of the personal luxury car. When he took over Chevrolet, he pursued the concept in the form of the Monte Carlo.

Pontiac's John DeLorean, who was actively involved in the development of the Grand Prix when he headed that division, invested similar effort in the Monte Carlo when he was promoted to general manager of Chevrolet. His influence can be seen in the personalized and well-appointed interior—pillowy bucket seats with available center console divider, wood-grained trim for the dash, and a plethora of comfort and convenience options ranging from full instrumentation to power windows and door

locks and electric rear defroster grid. The knightly crest of Monte Carlo rode proudly in the center of the egg-crate grille.

It was a more elegant car than the smaller, shorter, and rougher-looking Chevelle—but no less mean. Which is just the effect Chevy was after. Its menace burbled under the surface instead of splashing about noisily and obviously, like the Chevelle.

The Monte was a car for *men*—not hooligan twentysomethings.

Standard under the hood that first year was a two-barrel, 250-horsepower (SAE gross) version of Chevy's small-block V-8 with the buyer's choice of Powerglide two-speed or Turbo-Hydramatic 350 three-speed automatic.

You could add a four-barrel carb to the 350 and up the ante to 300 horsepower—or choose the torquey 400-cubic-inch small-block with two-barrel carb and 265 horsepower. The 400 was one of the biggest "small" V-8s Chevy (or anyone else) ever built. It looked the same externally as the normal Chevy small V-8 (283, 307, 327, 350) but had a non-interchangeable block with siamesed bores.

To beat up on teenagers in Chevelles and GTOs, one could always select the big-block 396 (which was now technically a 402). It bellowed out 330 horsepower and was ideally suited for the heavy-set Monte Carlo.

But when even that was insufficient, Chevy had more to offer. A Super Sport Package could be ordered for 1970 and 1971. It centered on the stupendous 454 V-8 tuned to 360 horsepower (365 in 1971) and a tire-annihilating 500 lb-ft of torque brutalizing the pavement through a THM400 three-speed automatic. In keeping with its more genteel image, manual transmissions were not teamed up with the 454 in the Monte Carlo SS. (Although there is an ongoing debate about the *possibility* of the four-speed having been available as an obscure Central Office Production Order, or COPO, special order.)

Also included as part of the SS package were a HD suspension with load-leveling feature, rear anti-sway bar, and performance 3.31 rear axle ratio.

As the baby boom generation matured, the market was ripe for a car like the Monte Carlo and Chevrolet sold a pile of them.

The first-generation Monte Carlos feature the longest hoods ever mounted to a mass-produced passenger car.

The SS Monte was only an intermittent offering, however. As the '70s rolled on, the Monte Carlo leaned ever more to the luxurious—and the large.

A redesign for 1973 accentuated the pontoon look, along with more roll to the overall shape, which seemed to be lunging forward, especially when viewed from the side. Fixed opera windows replaced the first-generation's rear quarter glass—and GM's new pull-up door handles had become standard equipment. The all-coil suspension was tuned for a soft, nautical ride; the cabin isolated from the road via six gel-soft rubber biscuits sandwiched between the frame and body. Radial tires were now standard, too.

Taking the same road pioneered by the personal Pontiac Grand Prix, the new Monte now featured a wraparound dash finished in burl walnut trim. The optional bucket seats swiveled to ease entry and exit. A sporty center console and floor shifter completed the ensemble. Chevy sold a cool quarter-million of them—and the '73 Monte was named Car of the Year by *Motor Trend* magazine.

Big-block power—in the form of a 235-horsepower 454—remained available, in addition to both two- and four-barrel versions of the 350- and 400-cubic-inch small-block V-8s. The 454 lasted through 1975 before being discontinued for the '76 models—which also got a revised front end treatment with stacked square headlights and new taillights. Though the '76 model was a bit awkward-looking and had far less power than the previous year, it turned out to be a monster hit for Chevrolet, with more than 400,000 sold. Many believe it was due to the fact that by this time, people were figuring out that big cars were on the endangered species list and that the Monte might not be around much longer.

It turned out that they were correct.

A two-thirds-scale third-generation Monte Carlo bowed for 1978. It had an exaggerated, forward canted front clip and an abbreviated bustle-back rear treatment that lacked the proportion and curb appeal of the earlier models. This was also the first year for V-6 power. Big-blocks were long gone and so was big horsepower. The largest V-8 available was the new 5.0-liter 305, ginning up a sad-sack 140 horsepower.

But all was not lost—yet, anyhow. In 1981, the Monte made a comeback with a new, NASCAR-inspired shape that resurrected the dignity of the earlier cars. It had the familiar long hood and handsome fixed rear quarter glass, but the overall proportions

Opposite: **By 1973,** DeLorean's original personal luxury coupe had morphed into a cocaine-fueled disco nightmare, complete with pontoon fenders and something marketed as an "opera window."

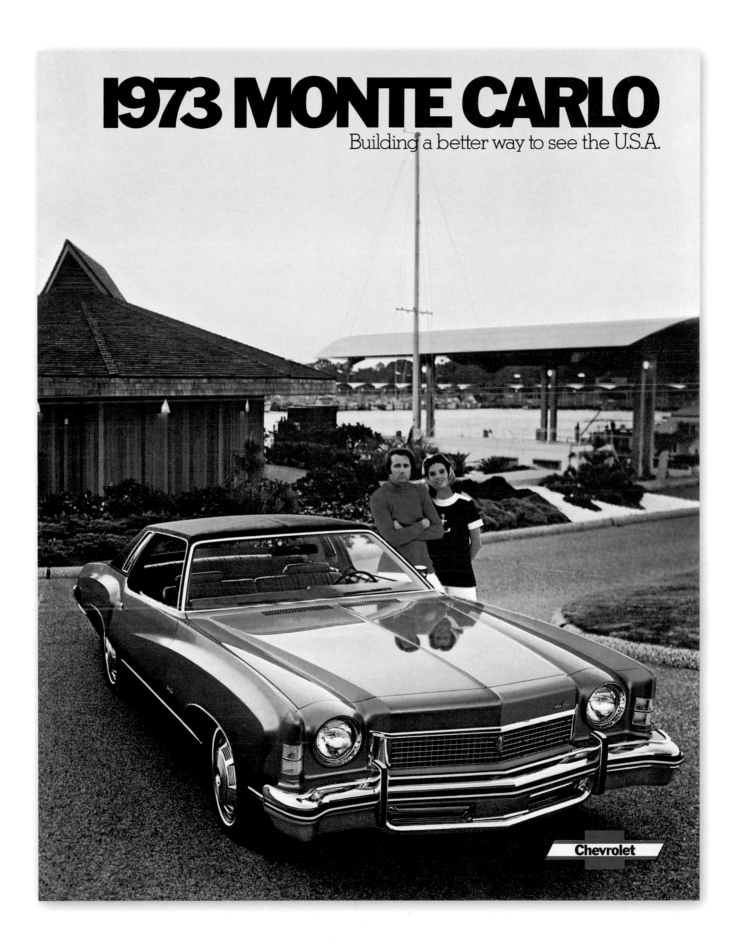

1973 MONTE CARLO

Building a better way to see the U.S.A.

Chevrolet

Chevrolet shrunk the Monte Carlo by 15 inches for the 1978 model year. In the new, smaller proportions, the car's elegant (if overwrought) styling went from baroque to toadlike.

Opposite top: **Chevrolet** cleaned up the styling of the Monte Carlo for the 1981 model year, replacing the drooping, toadlike haunches with clean, crisp sheet metal. All was forgiven when the division brought back the SS version, absent since 1971, for the 1983 model year.

Opposite bottom: **Since the Monte Carlo** was never offered as a convertible, open-air-motoring fans had to settle for leak-prone T-tops.

were vastly improved over the truncated 1978–1980 version. In 1983, the SS package returned, featuring monochromatic (all one color) paint, aero nose clip and—under the hood—the same L69 5.0-liter high-output V-8 that was offered in the Camaro Z28. It featured a Corvette camshaft, performance-calibrated carburetor, and low-backpressure exhaust. Tire-chirping 1–2 upshifts were back! The SS Monte Carlo offered performance comparable to the smaller Camaro, with usable back seats, a generous trunk, and far more comfortable seating up front.

The SS was a big hit, and by 1984, Chevrolet had sold close to 150,000 examples of all versions of the Monte Carlo.

In 1987, an Aerocoupe submodel appeared that was basically an SS with a convex rear glass and abbreviated deck lid. These were very low production compared with the standard SS and today are considered very collectible.

The year 1988 would be the last for a rear-drive Monte Carlo—though the name was revived in the mid-1990s for the Lumina coupe and continued through 2007. While V-8 power would make another comeback in 2006, the modern Monte just wasn't the same. Connoisseurs regard front-drive, downsized Monte Carlos as distant cousins of the Great Knight, at best.

Monte Carlo: Things to Know

Reportedly, the 1970 Chevrolet Monte Carlo was almost named Concours.

Model '70 SS 454 Monte Carlos are rare; records indicate that only 3,823 were manufactured. Models from 1971 are even more rare; only 1,919 were built before the SS package was cancelled. However, a detuned 454 V-8 remained available through 1975.

The '77 Monte Carlo, though technically listed as an intermediate-size car, was actually larger than the full-size Caprice that year.

Fourth-generation (1981–1988) Monte Carlos are the only Monte Carlos that were available with factory-installed glass T-tops.

A version of the 1983–1988 SS Monte Carlo was sold in Mexico with a less powerful, 165-horsepower engine of the 5.0-liter V-8 and other differences, including the regular sport coupe's wheels.

Monte Carlo SS.
Special Performance Edition.

Monte Carlo SS is a car that will impress you the instant you turn the key and hear that beautiful High Output V8 thunder into life. Here's driving excitement the way it was meant to be, with sophisticated engine and suspension componentry enveloped in an aerodynamically sleek shape. You get F41 Sport Suspension, dual exhausts, road-gripping Eagle GT white-lettered radials, rear spoiler,

power front ventilated disc brakes, quick recirculating-ball steering, sport steering wheel, full gage package with tach and special race-blue interior, all standard (for more details, see back cover). Behind the wheel you're surrounded by those personal touches that make any Monte Carlo such a satisfying car to own. In fact, the only thing about the car that won't blow you away is the price.

Monte Carlo SS 5.0 Liter High Output Engine	
Cylinder block, heads	Cast iron
Inlet manifold	Aluminum
Displacement	5.0 Liter (305 CID)
Horsepower	180 at 4800 RPM
Torque	235 lbs.-ft. at 3200 RPM
Compression ratio	9.5:1 with electronic spark control
Carburetion	4-Bbl. Rochester quadrajet
Valve train	Pushrod, hydraulic lifters
Valve diameter	1.84" inlet, 1.50" exhaust
Comshaft duration	320° inlet, 320° exhaust
Comshaft lift	.410" inlet, .423" exhaust
Crankshaft	Cast nodular iron, five main bearings
Exhaust system	Low restriction, dual, 2" front pipes, smooth (laminar) flow inlet wide-mouth monolith converter, dual 2¼" rear pipes with dual mufflers.

Monte Carlo SS standard race-blue interior. Bucket seats, shown next page, are also available.

GM Wind Tunnel test results. Cd · .375

NEW FUEL-INJECTED HEART. PULSE-QUICKENING STYLE.

The heart of Monte Carlo's performance is its new Electronic Fuel Injection 4.3 Liter standard V6 engine. Electronic Fuel Injection precisely delivers fuel for instant acceleration. And the on-board computer monitors and controls the process, measuring the incoming air and metering the fuel mixture and engine load, fine-tuning the engine up to 00 times a second for excellent performance.

Monte Carlo's pulse-quickening style is sculpted to cut through the wind and turn heads wherever it goes. And you can personalize it further with the optional removable glass roof panels, bucket seats, sport console, Sport mirrors and aluminum wheels shown here. Monte Carlo's power steering takes only 3.3 turns lock to lock for maneuverability.

The power front disc brakes are air vented for rapid cooling. And the 14" steel-belted radial tires are all-season M+S-rated (Mud and Snow), designed for low noise, long wear and excellent traction.

BAROQUE PSEUDO MUSCLE
LAGUNA 1973-1976

The mid-1970s were a weird and dangerous time for the American car industry. It had to turn on a dime—literally—and figure out how to compete with Japanese automakers that had no problem dealing with the sudden uptick in gas prices caused by various OPEC oil embargoes because all they sold at the time were small cars. Detroit, meanwhile, still had mostly traditional-sized, body-on-frame behemoths conceived in the '60s that assumed '60s-era conditions would last much longer than they did. Since they couldn't just throw away the cars they had, they had to figure out a way to make them work under the new regime.

A prime example of this is the short-lived Laguna series, which ran for just three years between 1973 and 1976.

The Laguna was named after the California racetrack (Laguna Seca) and was essentially a modified Chevelle with GM's attractive Colonnade styling defined by a

With performance no longer a selling point, the Super Sport version of the Chevelle no longer occupied the top rung on the model's hierarchical ladder. That spot was given to the Laguna package.

LAGUNA

Laguna. The New Top of the Line Chevelle with a Look all its Own.

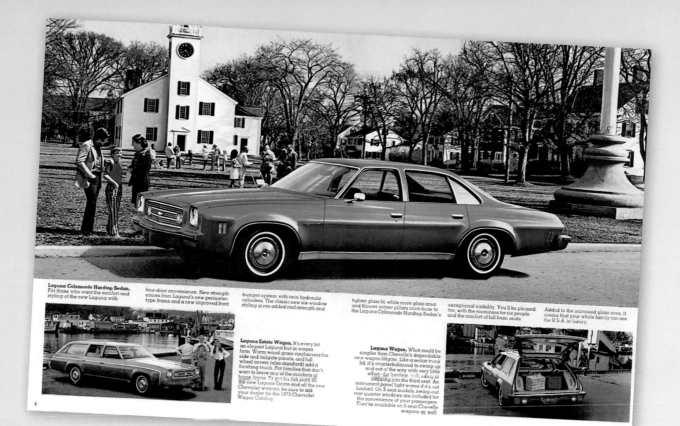

Laguna Colonnade Hardtop Sedan. For those who want the comfort and styling of the new Laguna with four-door convenience. New strength comes from Laguna's new perimeter-type frame and a new improved front bumper system with twin hydraulic cylinders. The classic new six-window styling gives added roof strength and tighter glass fit, while more glass area and thinner corner pillars contribute to the Laguna Colonnade Hardtop Sedan's exceptional visibility. You'll be pleased, too, with the roominess for six people, and the comfort of full foam seats. Added to the increased glass area, it means that your whole family can see the U.S.A. in luxury.

Laguna Estate Wagon. It's every bit an elegant Laguna but in wagon form. Warm wood-grain vinyl covers the side and tailgate panels, and full wheel covers (also standard) add a finishing touch. For families that don't want to leave any of the comforts of home, home. To get the full story of the new Laguna Estate and all the new Chevrolet wagons, be sure to ask your dealer for the 1973 Chevrolet Wagon Catalog.

Laguna Wagon. What could be simpler than Chevelle's dependable new wagon liftgate. Like a sedan trunk lid, it's counterbalanced to swing up and out of the way with very little effort—for loading with ease or stepping into the third seat. An instrument panel light warns if it's not latched. On 3-seat models, swing-out rear quarter windows are included for the convenience of your passengers. They're available on 2-seat Chevelle wagons as well.

sporty-looking, forward-raked B-pillar and fixed-glass rear quarter window that fed back into a fastback roofline.

The Colonnade look was actually a clever solution to a very real engineering problem: how to impart sufficient structural strength to a coupe's roof so as to meet the federal government's new (but never implemented) roof crush standards.

The Laguna also had a unique front-end treatment with one of GM's first fully integrated front fascias. Instead of the usual bolt-on bumper, the Laguna had a wraparound front clip made of color-matched flexible urethane plastic—GM called it Enduraflex—that integrated most of the formerly separate front-end items into a single unit. This presaged the design ethic that would become industry standard by the late 1980s, when bolt-on chrome bumpers were relics of the automotive past. But in 1973, the monochromatic look was highly unusual and the Laguna really stood out.

Inside, Chevy borrowed the Monte Carlo's swiveling front buckets (bench seats could also be ordered) and boasted nicer materials and trim unique to this model. The gauge cluster was a semiwraparound design, with all the controls oriented toward the driver.

A sharp-looking center console (with the buckets) canted forward, as if ready for action. And unlike the pony cars, a Laguna's interior was a rumpus room of open space. Even six-footers could occupy the rear seats—which are mostly unendurable in modern sporty coupes.

V-8 power was standard, too—which put the Laguna a notch above the econo-oriented Malibu (which came standard with an inline six) and just under the still-potent SS Chevelle.

Chevy management probably realized that the SS would soon be gone—and rather than keep the SS name on a gelded Chevelle, turned to the idea of the new Laguna as a kind of euro-themed American GT. It would still be big—and reasonably powerful—but not so over-the-top that survival would be impossible in the era of high-priced unleaded regular and catalytic converters.

The standard engine for 1973 would thus be a 350 two-barrel, offering 145 horsepower, working with a three-speed manual transmission. Buyers could step up to a four-barrel 350 and 175 horsepower offering—along with a four-speed manual or three-speed Turbo-

Government safety regulations forced designers to devise five-mile-per-hour bumpers that didn't look like chrome-plated railroad ties bolted to the front of cars. On the Laguna, Chevrolet's designers covered the apparatus with body-colored urethane material, creating a sleek-looking package.

Though Chevrolet advertised the Laguna S-3 as the "sportiest Chevelle," it was more of a personal luxury coupe, a Monte Carlo with sportier sheet metal.

Hydramatic. A mild-tune 454 four-barrel cranking out 250 horsepower was the Laguna's top engine—and when teamed with either the four-speed manual or the optional three-speed automatic, delivered credible performance with acceptable economy.

It may not have been an LS6 Chevelle SS 454—but it *was* close enough to keep the fires burning during a very dark period for the American auto industry.

Indeed, Chevy retired the Chevelle SS the following year, leaving the Laguna—which was now called Laguna S-3—as the division's only heavy-hitter. Sedan and wagons versions had been dropped—or rather, transferred back to the regular Malibu lineup.

For the final two years of its short life, the Laguna would be offered as hardtop coupe only.

It was during this period that the car came into its own as a kind of showroom stock stock car. A striking new shovelnose front-end treatment (along with the distinctive side louvers for the quarter windows and 15x7 Rally rims) gave it a 150-mile-per-hour look standing still. It seemed ready for Talladega as it sat—just add window netting and "76" decals on the door. And indeed, the actual stock car versions did very well on the super speedways of NASCAR—until NASCAR outlawed them!

Street versions now carried either a two-barrel 350 or an optional 400 four-barrel developing 180 horsepower. The 454 was still on the docket, too—though downrated slightly to 230 horsepower net.

Catastrophic converters—which became standard equipment across the GM lineup for the 1975 model year—meant the end for the 454, and even the 350 got pushed aside in favor of a new 305 small-block that shared the 350's stroke but had a smaller bore. It still managed 140 horsepower, even so—which was respectable in view of the fact that it had 45 fewer cubic inches than the '74 model's 350 two-barrel and also had to exhale through far more restrictive exhaust plumbing. The 400 four-barrel was the range-topper for 1976, managing 180 horsepower—which was, again, respectable in the context of the times. That year, for example, there was no Z28 Camaro—and the strongest engine you could order in the smaller F-car was a four-barrel 350 making all of 170 horsepower.

The Laguna was thus an interesting car when it was new and even more so today because you see them so infrequently. The side louvers and shovelnose front end still look custom, not factory—and owners often find themselves giving short history lessons about this unusual car, of which fewer than 20,000 total were ever made.

Right: **With the demise of the Super Sport,** the Type S-3 version of the Laguna became the top performance dog in the Chevelle lineup. The top engine option was a 454-cubic-inch monster producing just 230 horsepower (and even this shrunk to 215 horsepower over the years).

Below: **By the time** the Laguna Type S-3 disappeared from the lineup, the top engine option was just a 180-horsepower, 400-cubic-inch V-8. The neutered 454 had been put out of its misery.

Coupe de Ville: Things to Know

Oddly, while the Laguna's front end got the integrated, urethane fascia, the rear end still used a conventional bolt-on chrome bumper.

Two years after the production Laguna was cancelled by Chevrolet, NASCAR outlawed the use of Laguna-bodied stock cars.

Even though big-blocks were not available from the factory in 1976, the Laguna's cavernous engine compartment makes dropping one in a snap.

The famous quarter-window louvers were optional in 1974 but standard thereafter on coupes. A power-activated Skyroof sunroof and Landau vinyl roof were among the car's major optional extras.

One of the rarest Laguna variants is the '73 Laguna wagon with the 454 V-8 engine.

CHAPTER 4

OVER-THE-TOP LUXURY

Wretched Excess

**Cadillac Sedan deVille
Fleetwood Sixty and 75
Chrysler Imperial/New Yorker
Lincoln Continental**

CAPACIOUS
CADILLAC
SEDAN DEVILLE
1956-1984

In 1957, Cadillac's tailfins jutted up just slightly from the trunk. In 1958, they towered above it. For that year, the Sedan DeVille was offered only as a four-door hardtop.

Previous pages: **You say your luxury sedan** with the towering tail fins, each with taillight pods jutting out of them like a pair of jet-age erections isn't flamboyant enough for you? Well, paint it pink, then.

Luxury cars used to be all about relaxation. The modern concept of tightly fitted bucket seats, center consoles, and sport bike–like gauge pods would have seemed ridiculous to '70s-era Americans. They wanted weight. And glitz. And slide-across bench seats that may have offered exactly zero in the way of lateral support but that felt almost as cozy as your best TV-watching sofa back home. Fender skirts—and pop-off wire wheels. Column shifters—and plastic chrome.

You know . . . *the good stuff.*

In the modern era, all the really big sedans are foreign-made: Bentleys, Rolls-Royces, Daimler Maybachs. It is a sign of the decline of the once-magnificent American Land Yacht, whose last surviving exemplar (R.I.P. as of 2009) was the Lincoln Town Car—a mere middleweight by the standards that once defined full size.

Cadillac, for its part, doesn't make *truly* big cars anymore.

But once upon a time, wreath-and-crested mega-sedans ruled the roads. Of these, perhaps the best-known (and longest-lived) is the Sedan deVille, sister ship of the Coupe deVille, which remained more or less intact from its conception in the mid-1950s through 1984.

Like the coupe, the Sedan deVille was originally marketed as a high-trim version of the Series 62 and shared the 62's wheelbase, basic chassis, and most drivetrain components—including, initially, the 331- and 365-cubic-inch V-8s.

Cadillac placed it just under the mighty Fleetwood sedan, which at that time was a virtual custom-built exotic.

Over the ensuing years—and six generations of restyles and redesigns—the deVille sedan would become a common sight on American roads and a visible symbol of American upper middle class affluence. A deVille was, in its day, the equivalent of an Escalade EXT—only less ridiculous. After all, it was a road car—not an ersatz 4x4 fitted with the engineering equivalent of mechanical cod pieces in the form of boastful but never (or rarely) used off-road equipment.

The Sedan deVille boasted room for three abreast in each of its two rows of crushed velour bench seats, a trunk big enough to rent out to a family of illegals, and—during its prime years—the column-shifted wonderfulness of seven- and eight-liter V-8s feeding hungrily but quietly through 800 cfm Rochester Quadrajets, with linebacker-like torque sufficient to raise the prow two or three inches above the front whitewalls and hurling its bulk forward.

Amenities—such as air conditioning and power windows, which are givens in almost any modern car—were among the standard features that set a deVille apart from lesser cars back in the day. The side glass was frameless—and the action of the electric motors finger-pinching fast. Cadillacs were among the first GM cars to offer digital stereo radios, as well as the eight-track tape players (with specially made Cadillac music tracks ranging from Classical Gas to Burt Bacharach) and, later, CB radios, too.

Cadillac advertised the Sedan deVille as "The Predictable Winner"—and if the contest involved seeing how rapidly one could drain the 25-gallon tank, this was absolutely true. Nine MPGs was par; less if you leaned on it.

Color choices included Byzantine Gold (with complementary Medium Gold Dorian cloth interior), Medium Beige and Nottingham Green Firemist teamed with Sierra Grain White leather. Or choose Medium Blue Dubonnet cloth, if you prefer. Oriental Tamo Wood trim graced the dashboard and door panels—and of course, a *de riguer* option was the Bayberry vinyl-covered roof.

As one copywriter put it: "There is no more magnificent way to experience the spirit of the '70s than to view the world from behind the wheel of a 1970 Cadillac."

Probably the most impressive of the breed were the 1971–1976 versions, which were the biggest, offered the largest engines—including the 8.2-liter, 500 cubic-incher—the

THE NEW STANDARD OF THE WORLD IN DISTINCTION!

Sedan de Ville (Six Window)

Splendor is the constant companion of the owner of this supremely gracious version of the Sedan de Ville. Its advanced features of engineering and construction provide the most satisfying performance and superb comfort ever achieved in Cadillac's fifty-seven years of fine car leadership. And here, too, are all the elegant luxuries that have won for the Cadillac de Ville models the admiration of motorists everywhere. Interior selections are, of course, the same in all three distinguished de Ville creations.

Cadillac offered 11 different body styles for the 1959 model year, most of which were based on the Series 62 platform. The DeVille models were the most luxurious, and Sedan DeVilles were available as either four-window versions (hardtops with formal rooflines) or six-window versions, which had a sleeker rear design.

The Sedan de Ville FAMILY SIZE LUXURY.

There are many reasons why the DeVilles are perennially among America's most popular luxury cars. Start with four-door Cadillac roominess and comfort. Add to that DeVille elegance...and ride. And long-lasting value. This year, there's even more. New convenience features that are standard . . . the Freedom™ Battery that never needs water is just one. And new features you may specify...such as door locks that automatically lock when you place the shift lever in "Drive", a Fuel Monitor System, Cruise Control and Sunroof.

Unlike the other full-size General Motors sedans of the early 1970s, which often seemed bloated and oversize, the Sedan DeVille wore its girth well.

largest displacement V-8 Cadillac ever made. Seeing one of these beasts rolling up behind you in the rearview mirror could be unsettling. The four round headlights stared you down like the eyes of a Great White, with the gaping grille very effectively reminding you of the predator's glistening and razor-sharp teeth.

Two-hundred–pound chrome bumpers with battering ram vertical bumperettes promised devastating results to any who dared joust with one—except perhaps the owner of another deVille. These cars, at their high tide (1975–1976) measured 231 inches long and weighed more than 5,100 pounds—*without* driver or passengers. *With* four people on board and a few things in the trunk, 6,000 pounds of mass was brought to bear—commercial vehicle territory by modern downsized standards.

Naturally, things this large were destined not to live long lives. In 1977, Cadillac chopped nearly a foot of length and an astonishing 1,000 pounds off the flanks of the Sedan deVille. This version—which would continue through 1984—nonetheless actually boasted a slightly larger passenger compartment and trunk. Caddy designers simply reduced the front and rear overhangs to achieve the smaller overall profile. These latter-day deVilles were more boxy and stodgy than their predecessors but did achieve a certain notoriety as pimpmobile fodder, as well as conveyances for the well-heeled senior citizen set. They were also among the first of Cadillac's modern cars to benefit from the new overdrive automatic transmissions that became available in 1981.

Scads of these were built, too.

From 1977 to 1979, annual sales always tickled six figures. It was only in 1980 that things began to really slide—perhaps because of serial disasters under the hood, ranging from (egads!) the first modern use of a V-6 engine in a full-size Cadillac to the now-infamous diesel 350 that poisoned American buyers on this type of engine for decades to come. The big car's handsome shell remained, but the guts had become utterly gutless.

Things drifted along through 1984—after which the deVille became a front-wheel-drive compact unworthy of the wreath and crest. This lasted until the '94 model year, when a larger, but still four-wheel-drive—and oddly proportioned—deVille made a final try at a comeback. But as with most such attempts, you can't go back. The final, trickled-out remnant found employment as government staff cars and funeral home stiffie wagons.

When the last of them were made in 1999, few even noticed the passing—or shed a tear at the loss. The *real* deVille had already been dead for 15 years.

Cadillac designers capitalized on the public's fascination with space in the early 1960s and designed cars that looked more like fighter jets than earthbound land-transportation modules. Don't stand too close to that taillight nacelle lest the driver hit the afterburner button and you are engulfed in flames.

SEDAN DE VILLE

Here's the car that combines family-size roominess and four-door convenience with traditional De Ville luxury and value.

Electronic level control is included in De Ville's long list of standard features. Complementing De Ville's smooth ride is the smooth performance of the HT 4100 V8 with Digital Fuel Injection. Or a Diesel V8 is available at no additional charge. Sedan de Ville shown in Grayfern with available matching full vinyl roof.

Sedan deVille: Things to Know

The French appellation "deVille" loosely translates as "of the town."

Sedan deVille offered one of the first factory-installed air bag systems in 1974. The option was not popular, however, and only lasted two years.

A d'Elegance appearance package also made its debut for 1974 and included crushed velour seat covers, thick pile carpeting, and other trim upgrades. This package lasted much longer than the air bags, all the way through 1984 when the last of the traditional Sedan deVilles were built.

The year 1977 was the first that throttle body fuel injection was offered in place of a carburetor.

In 1980, for the first time in nearly 40 years, a six-cylinder engine was available in the deVille series as a credit option.

Cadillac celebrated its 75th anniversary in 1977 by shrinking most of its cars. This move was necessary to compete in an increasingly fuel-economy-minded auto market. The 1977 Sedan DeVille was nearly a foot shorter and 1,000 pounds lighter than the 1976 version. Likewise, the 500-cubic-inch V-8 shrunk to a mere 425 cubic inches.

FLEETWOOD
SIXTY SPECIAL AND 75
1946-1984

THE NEW *Cadillac — Fleetwood*

For those well-heeled customers who couldn't make do with a pedestrian Cadillac sedan, the division offered the Fleetwood, available as the Series 60 Fleetwood sedan (which was four inches longer than the Series 62 sedan sold to the hoi polloi) and the Series 75 Fleetwood limousine.

There is only one car that can outdo a classic Cadillac Kahuna when size matters—and that would be *another* Cadillac.

Specifically, the *ultimate* Cadillac—a Fleetwood Sixty or 75 Limo.

Preferably, a Brougham. (These were even *more* luxurious, if such a thing could be said.)

The *smaller* ones rode on 133-inch wheelbases. Limo versions ran to more than 151 inches from axle centerline to axle centerline and weighed close to 5,900 pounds empty.

No ordinary garage could handle this mechanical magnum.

Its gas tank held 27 gallons of leaded premium; you could enjoy a cup of coffee while the pumps strained to fill 'er up. Made for titans of industry, high-up politicians,

To get a sense of the massiveness of these rides, consider that an early 1970s model was capable of pulling a 7,000-pound trailer. This was a passenger car, remember. In the modern era, the only vehicles capable of pulling that kind of load are heavy-duty trucks and SUVs. A good tow rating for a modern car is 3,500 pounds—less than half what a Fleetwood in its prime was capable of dealing with.

FLEETWOOD BROUGHAM SEDAN

Here is traditional Cadillac luxury in the proud Fleetwood tradition. This prestigious automobile combines undeniable elegance and spacious comfort with advanced technology and Cadillac quality.

The standard full vinyl roof incorporates a special limousine-style rear window treatment, complementing the limousine-style ride. The smooth HT 4100 V8 with Digital Fuel Injection is standard.

Or you may opt for the 5.7 liter Diesel V8 at no additional charge. Fleetwood Brougham Sedan shown in Georgian Silver with matching full vinyl roof.

It lasted until 1984—the year Fleetwood, too, succumbed.

As with other storied Cadillac nameplates like Eldorado, rather than be permitted a soldier's death the decision was made to exploit the legacy and continue hawking the Fleetwood name as a marketing gimmick on smaller, front-drive pretenders—the longest of which just barely nosed ahead of the old Seville—in its time considered the compact Cadillac.

Early Fleetwoods, especially Broughams and those optioned out with the Talisman luxury appointments, were never built in large numbers, so they are pretty scarce today. But if you find one, snap it up. Restored to showroom condition, a Fleetwood Sixty or 75 in your (extra large) garage is the closest you'll ever come to owning your very own Iowa-class gunboat.

The Cadillac Fleetwood was the last of the original road hogs. By 1984, large, opulent American luxury cars had been replaced by econobox-derived, front-wheel-drive sardine cans.

Fleetwood: Things to Know

Silent screen–era heartthrob Rudolph Valentino owned a coach-built Fleetwood.

When even Fleetwood wasn't quite enough, buyers could always add on the optional Brougham d'Elegance package, which meant the car would be fitted out with extra-plush upholstery and carpets and special interior and exterior trim—including carpeted, drop-down footrests.

Fleetwood 75 limos were often modified for service as presidential limos, with armor-plated glass and other "classified" features.

In addition to being the last of the really big Cadillacs, Fleetwood had one of the last big V-8s—a 368 cubic-incher that survived through 1984. Lesser models had to make due with 350-cubic-inch and even 249-cubic-inch (HT4100) V-8s.

Just over 1,000 Fleetwood 75 limos were made in the final year.

CHRYSLER'S KING OF THE ROAD
IMPERIAL & NEW YORKER
1955-1982

Chrysler began using the *Imperial* nameplate for its top-of-the-line cars in the 1920s. In 1956, Chrysler spun the Imperial line off as its own separate division, a step above Chrysler in the corporate hierarchy.

The Southampton models were the most luxurious in the new Imperial division. Southamptons were available as both two-door hardtops and four-door hardtops.

Chrysler, alas, is no more. At least, it will never be the same—even if, by some miracle, the bankruptcy and reorganization manages to preserve the existence of the name in some form or other. The cars themselves are doomed—and in truth, have been gone since the early '80s, when the company went through its original death spiral. After that, it was K Cars and recycled and rebadged Benzes, never the Real Deal.

No, if you wanted the genuine article, you had to step back in time to the early Reagan era and before—when full-blooded Chryslers still emerged from the plant, proudly wearing the Pentastar on their ample flanks, baroque-scripted nameplates glued to their fenders—and Lean Burn V-8s gurgling under their hoods.

Come back to the fold, friend—and take a tour of what once was and never will be again.

There's a reason it's known as the Empire State.

New York is outsized and audacious—not a place for the timid. So is the car named after the Big Apple. It's a true giant that traces its origins all the way back to the 1930s, when it was introduced as an option package on the range-topping Imperial.

Features such as a FirePower Hemi V-8 gave the 1950s versions unprecedented power—while a wheelbase of 126 inches (by 1955) endowed it with proportions that assured it would leave an impression wherever it went. Literally. The thing was more than heavy enough to crinkle soft asphalt—or sink to its chrome doorsills in your neighbor's grass if you dared drive it that far.

During the mid- to late 1950s, Chrysler continued to develop the New Yorker as a kind of high-status automotive intimidator, with the optional Hemi-headed V-8 having swelled to 392 cubes and more than 300 horsepower (for 1957) feeding through a new and fully modern Torqueflite three-speed automatic operated via a toggle-style PowerFlite gear selector.

These cars could reach 60 in ten seconds—a fierce sprint for the time. Chrysler's torsion bar front suspension, meanwhile, gave the car a nautical feel as it plowed through the corners, lurching this way and that.

Nineteen fifty-seven was also the year Chrysler's new Forward Look styling—the brainchild of Virgil Exner—made its appearance. Fans of the movie *Christine* will be familiar with this menacing apparition. The New Yorker was essentially a dressed-up

The Imperial proved the ideal platform to show off Virgil Exner's elegant designs for the 1956 model year. Many people consider these cars a high-water mark in the art of automotive design.

THE NEW YORKER *4-door hardtop*

For those who wanted Chrysler luxury but couldn't quite afford an Imperial, Chrysler offered the New Yorker.

Like the Imperial, the New Yorker received sharper, more angular styling for the 1957 model year.

Fury (subject of the movie) with more luxury but the same fearsome jutting tail fins and glowering front-end treatment. Exner got the nickname Virgil *Excess* in part because of the over-the-the-top styling of the '57s.

But, none can deny they were arresting cars—every bit "body by Plymouth [or Chrysler, as the case may be] and soul by Satan." The Forward Look would last only four years, though, through the '61 model year.

The mid-1960s versions of the New Yorker lost the outsized fins and (for a while) the optional Hemi V-8, settling into a temporary quiescence as Chrysler's not-too-obstreperous high-line large sedan/coupe. The rather ornate-looking Electro-luminescent 1962–1964s (with the oddball V quad headlights) gave way to a more pleated—and low and wide—look for 1965–1968. Convertible coupes and wagons were available during this era, in addition to the big sedans.

New Yorker's wheelbase actually got trimmed back by two inches during this period, too—though the car was still a presence to be reckoned with. A Golden Lion 413-cubic-inch V-8 was available under the hood, too. At the time, a top-of-the-line Chrysler like New Yorker was considered the equal, or at least competitive with, the top-of-the-line luxury offerings of GM's Cadillac division and Ford's Lincoln division.

Then came 1974—and an all-new New Yorker that was the automotive equivalent of World War II's Battle of the Bulge. Like *Der Führer*'s desperate throwdown in the

An extra-large rear window highlights the beauty of this new New Yorker 2-Door Hardtop—below in deep-hued Bluegrass.

THE DRAMATIC NEW YORKER! Supreme achievement of Chrysler craftsmanship set boldly apart by its insert air-scoop grille and the richest interiors ever fitted to a New Yorker. Spectacular power, unusual economy. Rugged, silent Unibody construction. For the man who wants luxury and spaciousness mated to spirit and youth.

You lead the parade in this New Yorker 4-Door Hardtop—finest of all Chryslers. Dress it in Terra Cotta—a new hue for this new car—or choose from a palette of 18 other colors.

The New Yorker featured more subdued styling than the Imperial. This would prove to be a good thing.

Those buyers for whom the staggeringly tall tailfins weren't outrageous enough could buy the optional fake spare tire bulge that completed the big-pimpin' look.

Chrysler's design chief, Virgil Exner, went a bit wacky on the styling of the 1960 Imperial, giving the car exaggerated features like headlights set in floating pods, hooded headlights that had the appearance of a furrowed brow, and even a vaguely square steering wheel. Still, the car sold well.

People either loved or hated the 1961 Imperial Crown convertible, but they certainly couldn't ignore it.

winter of '44, Chrysler decided to bring forth a New Yorker with more steel, more engine, and more sheer bulk than any before.

It was the kind of car you needed to step back from by at least 10 yards to get into your camera's viewfinder—nearly 232 inches long and sleek like the flanks of a B-29 Superfortress. An upright, waterfall-style grille was flanked on either side by hidden headlight doors and thin-line vertical parking lamps. Sedans had frameless door glass and a pillarless look that was supremely elegant. In chocolate brown with a tan vinyl roof and royal tufted red velour upholstery (Corinthian Leather was optional), a fender-skirted, white-walled New Yorker was truly a regal spectacle.

Loaded examples easily cost in excess of $10,000, or about twice the cost of a family-priced Chevy sedan.

Lift the acre-size hood and behold 440 cubic inches under a twin-snorkel air cleaner—the same basic engine as the highway patrol got in their stripped-down

The styling of the early 1960s Imperials may have been odd, but it resulted in a striking automobile.

THE IMPERIAL LE BARON

This is, by all measures, the most exclusive car now being made in America. You won't see the LeBaron on the streets in great numbers, simply because a car of such integrity and excellence can't be produced by the usual production-line methods. ■ Every inch of every LeBaron is closely inspected for the tiniest flaws before a drop of paint is applied. ■ Its interiors are individually hand cut and hand fitted with the world's finest broadcloths and leathers, in a carefully keyed array of colors. ■ Its luxuries include, as standard equipment, just about every convenience yet invented for automobiles. ■ Its "town car" rear window is not only a handsome styling distinction, but it affords welcome privacy to passengers. ■ The LeBaron is the finest of America's most carefully built cars.

STANDARD EQUIPMENT. Power vent windows. Power window lifts. Six-way power seat. Constant-Control power steering. Total-Contact power brakes. TorqueFlite automatic transmission with pushbutton drive selector. Dual headlamps. Air-foam padded seat cushions, front and rear. Full-volume air-foam seat backs, front and rear. Center arm rest, front and rear. Padded safety steering wheel. Safety cushion instrument panel. Panelescent instrument lighting. Carpet floor covering. Vanity mirror. Outside left rearview mirror. Tilt-type interior rearview mirror. Interior lights actuated by front and rear doors. Map light. Luggage compartment light. Back-up light. Hand brake warning signal. Step-on parking brake. Variable-speed electric windshield wipers. Windshield washer. Electric clock. Cowl fresh-air intake. Four-barrel carburetor. Full-flow oil filter. Ultra-fine fuel filters. Aluminized dual exhausts. Landau roof with stainless steel insert. Wheel opening, stone shield and sill moldings. Factory undercoating and hood insulation pad. Tubeless white sidewall tires. Safety-rim wheels.

Imperial's flawless finish is achieved by patient inspection of each body in raw metal, then by hand sanding of every coat but the final one. Hand sanding takes extra time in production, but it achieves a finish no machine has yet been able to match.

The 1961 LeBaron is fitted out in the most elegant selection of fabrics and leathers of any car in America. A total of nine combinations of materials and colors is available. You choose from all broadcloth, all leather and combinations of broadcloth and leather. New carpeting material, especially developed for Imperial, retains its beauty up to twice as long as conventional automobile carpeting.

Imperial LeBaron four-door Southampton in Formal Black with stainless steel Landau Roof

The styling of the early 1960s Imperials didn't get any less odd when viewed from behind. The drooping trunk exaggerated the already exaggerated height of the tailfins. The truly strange could order a fake spare tire bulge for the trunk lid.

Newports and Furys. And *those* were honest 150-mile-per-hour cars—despite the aerodynamic profile of a cinder block and just a three-speed transmission with no overdrive. Think Bluesmobile—only with every power and creature feature Chrysler could throw into the mix, from vanity mirrors to a six-way power seat to tilt and telescoping (even leather-covered in 1977) steering wheel to a power radio mast and remote-control trunk opener.

Twelve miles per gallon on a good day, if you were lucky, but who cared? It was a life-affirming privilege in those dreadful downsized days to captain a New Yorker.

Unfortunately, Chrysler brought forth this behemoth at the absolute worst possible moment—just in time for the aftershocks of the 1973 OPEC oil embargo. Much as Americans still pined for full-scale pavement pounders, gas lines and escalating gas prices were forcing a reality check. External factors ensured that the '74 New Yorker would be not just one of the largest Chryslers ever but also among the last of its kind. Within five years, things would change significantly. Coupe versions of the New Yorker were also soon to be extinct. They were discontinued when the '79 R Bodies appeared and the New Yorker got downsized. From 1979 forward, New Yorker would be offered in sedan form only.

The 440 (and 400) V-8s were history as well. But the 318 and 260 V-8s did survive through 1981.

The year 1982 was the end of the line—not for the name, but definitely for the idea. The K-car-based '83 New Yorker was what the times demanded, but this front-wheel-drive, four-cylinder-powered compact was as far-removed from large-living New York as a walkup flat in Jersey.

The Imperial's sister car, the Chrysler New Yorker, adopted more daring style in the late 1960s, with fastback rooflines and scooped-out side panels.

Opposite: **In the mid-1960s** Imperial designers took a 180-degree turn and went from the dramatic (some might say "bizarre") to the conventional, with simple, angular lines that lent themselves well to the elegant Imperial Crown Coupe.

A superb example of automotive excellence, this is the Imperial LeBaron Crown Coupe.

New Yorker: Things to Know

The FirePower Hemi V-8 first appeared in the '51 New Yorker (and Imperial), displacing 331 cubic inches and producing 180 horsepower. It was one of the most powerful production engines of its time.

A St. Regis option package endowed the New Yorker with two-tone paint and other trim/cosmetic enhancements similar to the Cadillac Brougham package offered on Coupe deVille and other models.

Chrysler's Lean Burn carburetors of the 1970s helped to reduce emissions but created serious drivability problems, especially at cold start.

Chrysler was one of the first automakers to offer a five-year/50,000-mile warranty—and did it back in 1963.

The 1974 New Yorker was actually first to offer the notorious Corinthian Leather made famous by the Cordoba in 1975.

Opposite: **Chrysler introduced** one last generation of the original full-size Imperial in 1974. Unfortunately, American consumers had lost interest in massive cars because of rising gas prices, and Chrysler sold just over 14,000 units.

The last-generation Imperials survived just two model years. In 1975, Chrysler sold less than 9,000 units and pulled the plug on its long-running luxury series.

The Imperial LeBaron Four-Door Hardtop is distinguished by its formality, accepted for its elegance.

LARGE-LIVING LINCOLN
CONTINENTAL
1970-1979

PHOTOGRAPHED on a dock at Coronado Cays in Southern California, the four-door Lincoln Continental Town Car for 1975 presents a picture of stately beauty in a setting of fine ships. Traditionally the elegant luxury car of America, it is now more elegant than ever. Besides additional standard equipment and new engineering features for '75, the Lincoln Continental Sedan offers substantially new exterior

designs. The most dramatic of these is seen in the newly styled roof line. Though more changed in appearance than in any year since 1970, this four-door sedan remains an artistic example of understated contemporary beauty.

The distinctive new opera windows, with the Continental Star, suggest the aristocratic feeling one gets from the classic cars of decades ago, and, in the Town Car shown here, the coach

lamps on the pillar between the doors combine with the beautiful standard filigreed body side molding to contribute still more to an aura of tastefulness.

The Lincoln Continental interior is enhanced by a newly styled instrument panel which features a Cartier-signed digital clock, and the motif of the new upholstery sew style presents an appearance of sumptuous luxury and relaxing comfort.

...*Lincoln Continental Sedan*

Lincoln Continental Town Car

New opera window

Optional Town Sedan velour interior

Rear design with vertical tail lamps

Lincolns have always been large, luxurious cars, but the Continental, unveiled for the 1970 model year, took the brand's proportions to Rubenesque levels.

Lincoln, in the words of Brando, used to be a contender. For a time, it was neck and neck with GM's Cadillac division, the two sparring over who would be the number one luxury carmaker in the country. Brands like BMW, Mercedes-Benz, and Audi were quirky and foreign and, mostly, small. Lexus, Acura, and Infiniti were yet to come. This was still the high-sun era of the American car industry, and its stupendous steeds were the undisputed kings of the road.

Lincoln did some of its best work in this period, with the wide-glide Continental among its recognized masterpieces.

The Continental has appeared in various guises over the years—beginning its life in 1939 as a one-of-a-kind, hand-built custom made for the personal use of Edsel Ford—and ending up as a nothing-special front-wheel-drive failure by the late 1990s. In between were high-style models, such as the 1956–1957 Mark II, and, later, the iconic

...*Lincoln Continental Coupé*

Lincoln Continental Town Coupé

THE TWO-DOOR Lincoln Continental Coupé for 1975 is destined to join the illustrious line of automotive aristocracy that began with the first Lincolns in the early Twenties. It is very modern and very beautiful. It says as much about its owner as it says about itself—good taste is in evidence and the taste is obvious even though it doesn't shout.

The Lincoln Continental Coupés are truly distinctive. They have wide center pillars and large quarter windows of fixed glass into which the handsome Continental Star is laminated. The coach lamps on the center pillar are a distinguishing Town Coupé feature. The filigreed body side molding adds a touch of luxury as well as protection. From every exterior point of view, the Coupé has aesthetic elegance and majestic grace. Inside the Town Coupé is resplendant evidence of luxury, good taste and meticulous craftsmanship—invitations to enjoy the sumptuous comfort and quiet of the famed Continental ride.

New Town Coupé interior

Handsome new instrument panel

New quarter window and coach lamp

8

9

"JFK mobile" convertible sedan (available with both rear-hinged suicide doors and a Super Marauder 430-cubic-inch V-8) produced from 1961 until 1969.

But the Connie that super-sized all its predecessors—and which you'd be most likely to see in a remake of *Goodfellas*—appeared in 1970 and ran through 1979.

It was not only the biggest Lincoln—and the last big Lincoln—but it was the last really big luxury sedan to be laid down by an American automaker, period. By 1977, Lincoln stood alone—the others having thrown in the towel and accepted the new regime of calling formerly mid-size cars full size and hoping no one would notice.

They did, of course—but by then it was already too late. The deed was done.

Actually, the first hint of the '70 model came with the introduction, in 1968, of the brooding (and near 5,000-pound) Continental Mark III coupe. Lincoln used it to give the public a foretaste of the redesigned Continental full line (sedans as well as coupes) that would make its official debut the following year.

The Mark III had dramatic, knife-edged styling, and the monolithic look of a massive lead ingot, its slab-sided lines broken only slightly by the understated use of chrome accents. The sole exception to this motif was the forbidding, Rolls-Royce-inspired radiator shell. Sitting between the twin hidden headlamp doors, it dominated the landscape of the Connie's battering-ram front end. A thin-line bumper underneath seemed to be perfectly positioned to scrape up whatever debris was left after the tip of the car did its devastating work.

The roofline appeared low, even chopped, a visual trick achieved by the slimline C-pillars, which met the rear quarters several inches higher than the upper sill plate of the doors. Elliptically shaped opera windows that looked like Os that had been squeezed from the top and bottom enhanced the effect.

Though it seems inconceivable today, offering two-door coupe versions of three-ton land yachts seemed a reasonable proposition in the 1960s and 1970s. The doors on these vehicles were longer than the wheelbase of a modern Smart car.

The Collector's Series Lincoln Continental

At its peak, the Lincoln Continental measured 233.4 inches stem to stern.

The pièce de résistance, of course, was the spare tire bulge in the trunk—decorative by now but as iconic as ever—with L-I-N-C-O-L-N spelled out boldly in individual chrome lettering around the perimeter.

When the sedan version appeared, it shared these styling elements but rode on a longer, 126-inch wheelbase (versus 117.2 for the Mark III coupe), to be extended in 1971 to 127 inches and then again in 1974 to 127.2 inches.

Untold scenes of '70s-era car chases began with the driver of the chased car glancing fearfully into the rearview mirror at the sight of a black Continental closing rapidly.

There was go with the show, too—at least for the first few years. Lurking underneath that huge sheet of stamped-steel hood was the third-largest V-8 ever installed in an American car, the 460 big-block, complete with Autolite four-barrel carburetor, and it could travel 10 miles per gallon—EPA certified. Only Cadillac offered heftier lumps of cast iron (the 472-cube and 500-cube V-8s used in Eldorados), but Lincoln's lasted longer, through 1978—two full model years after GM retired all its really big engines, the 500 included.

For the first two years (1970 and 1971), the 460 was built with high-compression pistons and produced a very solid 365 horsepower. After 1971, power dropped to 224 horsepower (declining by a couple of horsepower each year after that until the lowest point, in 1976, was reached at just 202 horsepower). But while the huge V-8 may have lost its high-rpm punch, it excelled at producing locomotive-like torque at just off idle speed.

And the Connie needed every cubic inch of the 460's available thrust. This car had the biggest footprint of any mid- to late '70s-era capital ship, weighing in at close to 5,400 pounds (in 1974) and casting a near 20-foot shadow at the curb.

Standard-size garages often could not accommodate the beast.

It was as pimped out as it got, too. Standard accoutrements included thick, twenty-five-ounce cut-pile carpeting; a Cartier timepiece (not merely a *clock*); and six-way twin comfort lounge seats—finished in crushed velour or slide-as-you-go cowhide. Other amenities included lighted ashtrays for everyone, an AM/FM/MPX stereo, and a power sunroof. The breadbox-shaped dash housed an array of disco-era delights, including a bank of six idiot lights to the right of the rectangular speedo/clock/gas gauge combo.

After 1976, nothing approached its three key measures: length, wheelbase, or weight. And even though the 460 eventually got dropped (after 1978), the car itself still strode on its almost-unbelievable 127.2-inch wheelbase all the way through 1979 (with a still-credible 400-cubic-inch V-8 for motive power).

In an especially cruel twist of fate, the big Connie was still selling well when it got its walking papers. In fact, it was selling *better than ever.*

According to the records, 76,458 Continental sedans found homes (presumably, in oversize garages) in 1979—which was a not small uptick over the previous year's number, 67,110. Big love for big cars still burned bright, but the Connie was doomed, caught in the gunsights of the federal government's recently enacted Corporate Average Fuel Economy (CAFE) requirements, which required that each automaker's combined fleet of passenger cars average at least "X" MPGs or face a kneecapping in the form of onerous gas guzzler taxes to punish would-be buyers for their profligate ways.

So, although the Continental pleased the *market,* it did not please the *bureaucrats* in Washington—whose CAFE sword of Damocles twitched over the balding pates of Lincoln's senior management. They, in turn, took the sword to the Connie—reducing its weight by almost 900 pounds and cutting its overall length by nearly two feet in order to make the weasels in D.C. happy. But it was not a happy day for the Connie, whose sales immediately plummeted by almost two thirds to 24,056. Now that it had joined the downsized dregs of GM and Chrysler, it had lost its main draw—the fact that it been a *presence* unlike the rest.

Lincoln never really recovered—and the Connie's summary dry-docking can be seen as the beginning of this inexorable decline. The only bright spot through the 1980s was the Mark VII coupe—which boasted Mustang GT power, rear-drive, and the hunky good looks of an American SL450.

Meanwhile, the Connie shuffled off into obscurity—and by 1997 the jig was up at last.

From 1980 to the end, the government-approved CAFE Connie never came close to achieving the sales performance of the final run of *real* Connies, in 1979.

The public's collective cry, "Where's the beef?"—went unanswered.

But the good memories of better times will linger forever.

Continental: Things to Know

Lincoln's 1974 advertising brochure for the Continental described it as the car "that has become a legend in its own time."

Buyers could order a Cavalry Twill vinyl roof—in their choice of eight different colors.

Lincoln touted the high resale value of the Continental as one reason to buy it. Gas mileage was not mentioned as often.

The year 1977 was Lincoln's best to date, sales-wise, with Continental outselling the recently downsized Cadillacs for the first time ever.

For the final year of the full-size Continental, Lincoln offered a Collector's series version, which included nearly every available option and that pushed the car's base price to more than $20,000—an increase of some $8,000 over the base price of $11,200 that year.

The Williamsburg Town Car

Although all other brands were downsizing by the mid-1970s, Lincoln resisted and continued to produce the industrial-size Continental until 1979.

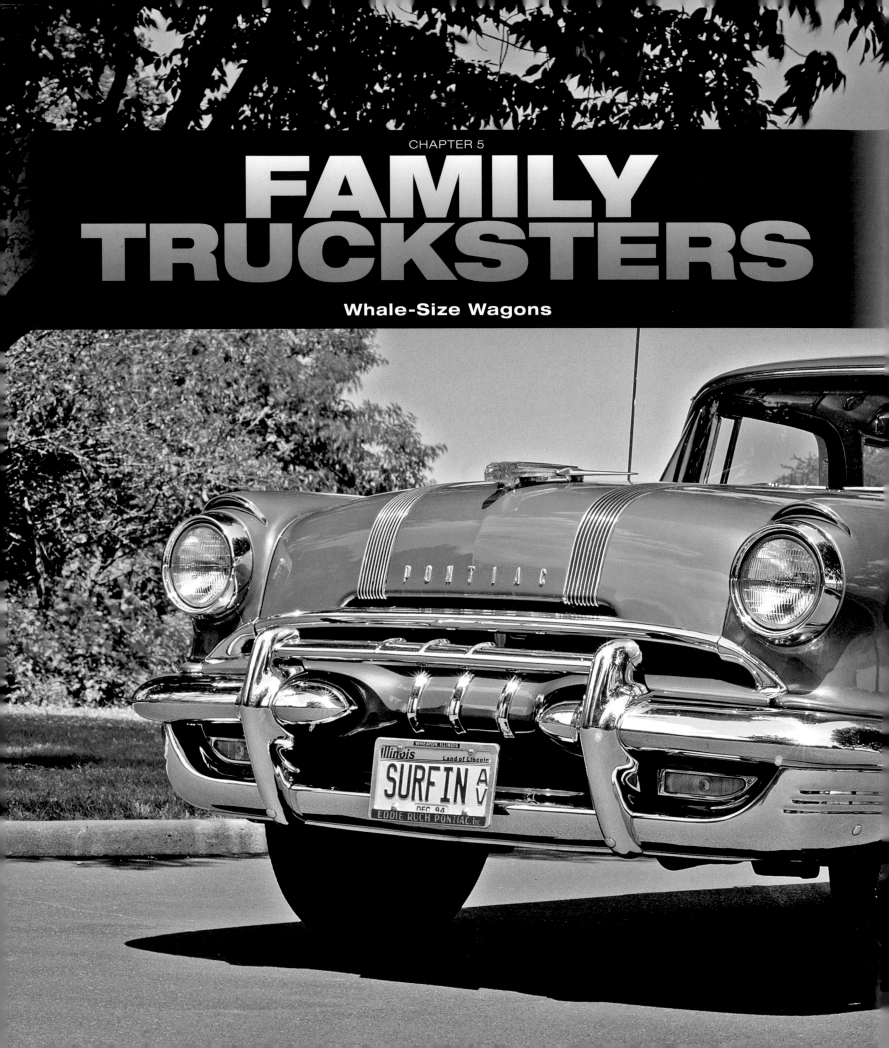

CHAPTER 5

FAMILY TRUCKSTERS

Whale-Size Wagons

Chevy Kingswood
Oldsmobile Vista Cruiser
Buick Estate Wagon
Ford Country Squire
Pontiac Safari

HEAVY CHEVY
KINGSWOOD ESTATE
WAGON
1969-1972

Chevrolet Wagon features put you in your place. First.

The only walk-in rear door in its field.

Here's what our walk-in is all about: an easy-to-reach boarding step right in the bumper; a dual-action tailgate door; and a swept-back roof design. All combine to let you walk in, stand up, turn around and sit down. There's no bending, no head-banging.

Look. hidden hinges.

There's a lot more here than meets the eye. We've completely concealed the tailgate hinges, which gives Chevrolet Wagons a neater, trimmer look. You won't snag your clothing. Or get bumped. One more thoughtful item: our door handle is on the inside. No one gets in without a key.

Chevrolet's third seat.

Some makers put side-facing rear seats in their wagons. We do an about face. Our third seat faces the rear. Why? Room. Room for people to sit together comfortably. No knee-knocking, no shoulder-hunching.

Side-guard beam.

We could call it your "security beam." A strong, steel guard beam built into the side of the body and doors of Chevrolet Wagons. We put over 40 pounds of guard-rail steel in there to strengthen both sides and provide a more solid wall between you and the outside world. Would you believe a lot of wagons in Chevrolet's field don't have it?

Several full-size humans could easily disappear into the cavernous rear compartment of the Chevrolet Kingswood wagon.

One of the greatest things about the Great Whales of the past was their names. Today, everything's alphanumeric: "X" this and "123" that. All the good names have either been taken, are owned by someone else, or couldn't be applied to a modern car without inciting rib-cracking laughter (or the ire of the political-correctness police). Take, for example, the Chevrolet Kingswood. Today the concept of the king's wood would have modern helicopter parents doing a St. Vitus dance as they tried to protect their precious snowflake children from the sordid images such a name would conjure. But in less cynical times, the Chevy Kingswood had much less sinister connotations.

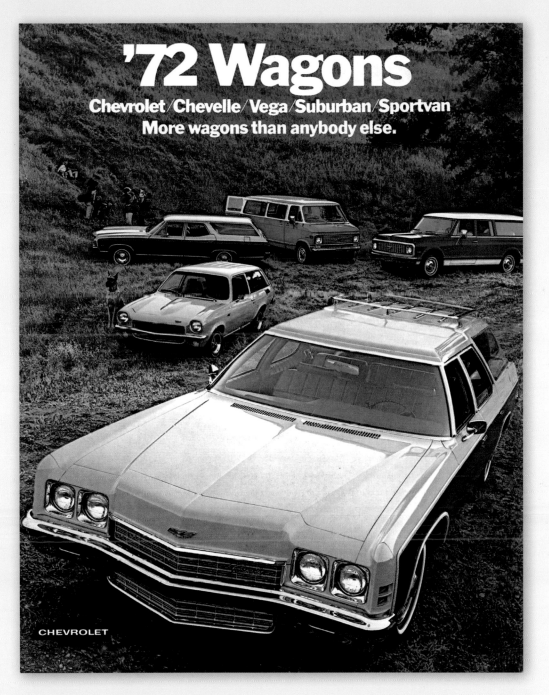

'72 Wagons

Chevrolet/Chevelle/Vega/Suburban/Sportvan
More wagons than anybody else.

CHEVROLET

Back in the days when men were manly enough to drive station wagons instead of tarted-up trucks with off-road pretensions, the full-size Chevrolet wagon was the ultimate utility vehicle.

Real wagons are long gone. Today's "crossovers" are just minivans in drag—or sports sedan wannabes. Many are quick, it's true, fully capable of doing figure eights around an old-school battlewagon in terms of what is known as "driving dynamics" in these, the latter days of the empire.

But it was not always so. A time existed when wagons weren't wimpy crotch-fruit conveyances—or SUVs suffering from an identity crisis. No all-wheel drive, no 21-inch rims, no flat-screen TVs or built-in child seats: just acres of steel and miles of chrome with rear-facing jump seats and no seat belts for the kiddies, who got to roll around like

Here's how the vanishing tailgate works.
To put it down. Turn the key to the right. The window slides up and into the roof. Another turn to the right and the gate drops down and slides under the floor with a gentle downward push. There's even a power-assisted gate available that lets you dispense with the gentle downward push.
To get it up. Just pull the gate up. You can do it with one hand, easily, because the gate is counterbalanced (the power gate goes up automatically when you turn the key). With the gate up, just turn the key to the left and the window slides back down. (For your fingers' sake, the power window will only lower part way unless the gate is closed first.)

A tailgate that's out of sight.
No gate. No door. No hinges. That's Chevrolet's Glide-Away tailgate. But to be honest, our vanishing act has raised a couple of questions.

First, is anything that looks that simple, really that simple? And second, who is it built for?

First question. Yes, it is that simple. The gate, which has very few moving parts, just glides down under the floor on two big steel tracks. We've even added a new manual switch so you can lower the gate without the key when the window is partly raised. The window and gate work with the ease and regularity of any power window. And because the rear end so no air deflector is needed. Aerodynamics help keep the window clean.

Second question. Who is it built for? People who don't need a tailgate. Now they can load without bending over a gate. Or they can load from both sides. Or in bumper to bumper parking. Or in a closed garage. Or, if hauling a boat or camper, they can unload without unhitching. The vanishing tailgate makes all those things possible.

You'll also like the space it leads to. Which, by the way, is considerable. 106.4 cubic feet to be specific. That's figured with the back seats down, going from the back of the front seat to the rear gate (100.5 inches long). But even as this picture shows, with all three seats up, there's room for gear behind the forward-facing third seat. It's like having a trunk on a three-seat wagon.

There's even a hidden compartment under the trunk floor. Now when you carry valuables like camera equipment, you've got the perfect place to put them. Out of sight.

Chevrolet Wagon.

The good old days, when you could just toss the kids in the back of the Family Truckster to bounce around with the laundry instead of strapping them in some NASA-approved titanium-reinforced safety module . . .

Estate Wagon: Things to Know

The 1969 Estate Wagon shared the same basic 119-inch wheelbase as the Impala sedan.

By 1972, the final year for the model series, the wheelbase had grown to a stupendous 125.1 inches.

A loaded '72 Estate Wagon with three-row seating carried a base price of $4,423 and weighed a scale-crunching 4,883 pounds.

Chevy ran an ad for the '60 Estate Wagon that showed a pop-up camper on the roof; it's unclear whether such equipment was ever offered as a factory (or dealer) option.

Six taillights provided ample illumination—and hinted at the Estate Wagon's Impala origins.

logs on the flat rear floor as the weight shifted around every corner.

It was an experience today's generation will never know, one that an earlier generation lived through in sheetmetal sauropods like Chevy's Kingswood Estate wagon.

The Kingswood Estate rode on GM's super battleship B platform, the same basic keel used from the mid-1960s through the mid-1990s, when the last of the line (in the form of Buick's Roadmaster/wagon and the Chevy Caprice/wagon) were finally given the needle.

Though GM (and Chevrolet) had built wagons before, models like the Kingswood would prove the fullest expression of the concept. In the late 1950s, the designation was applied to mid-trimmed wagon versions of the Bel Air, just under the well-known Nomad series. Beginning in 1969, the Kingswood designation migrated to the Impala lineup, where checking that option box meant you got a full-size wagon on the Impala's chassis with two or three rows of seats and standard V-8 power flowing to the rear whitewalls via a three-speed column-shifted manual transmission.

Buyers could order a power rear window or step up to the top-trim Kingswood Estate, which came with the power window included. Creature comforts abounded, from power windows and locks all around to cruise control and Freon-powered air conditioning that delivered meat-locker cold sufficient to frost the chrome-trimmed vents.

But the Kingswood's signature feature was the outward swinging rear gate—fully carpeted on the Estate—that provided access to the cavernous rear cargo (or kid-carrying) area. In those pre-seat-belt, booster-seat-free days, young 'uns were free to flop around back there protected against injury, not by air bags and ABS, but thick-cut steel. People under 40 with no direct recollection of these beasts cannot conceive how safe it felt to be cocooned deep within the armored embrace of these magnificent monsters. The distance from the edge of the rear doors to the back of the wagon was easily six feet. The sheets of glass used for the side panels were bigger than the fenders of a new Honda Accord.

Chevrolet's advertising from the period called them the "walk-in wagons"—and that was no kidding.

And they weren't just large on the outside. Buyers could choose from a full range of small- and big-block V-8s, all the way up to the same basic 396 V-8 that powered muscle coupes like the Chevelle. A few 427 wagons may have been built, too—and in any case, one would fit just as easily. Cars built in the 1970–1971 model years could be equipped with the even bigger 454 as well as dual exhaust and Positraction rear.

That's seven liters and 425 horsepower in a two-ton 20-footer.

Put *that* in your late-model V-6/FWD minivan and smoke it!

OLDSMOBILE ELEPHANT
VISTA CRUISER
1964–1977

OLDSMOBILE STATION WAGONS WHERE THE ACTION IS!

Introducing the all new VISTA-CRUISER

Here is a fact that some will find hard to swallow: GM's Oldsmobile division was once the number-three best-selling brand of car in the United States.

Believe it or not.

Given Oldsmobile's consumptive decline and sad demise at the dawn of the twenty-first century, it's hard to imagine a time when Oldsmobiles not only sold in vast fleets but were also very far indeed from the sad-sack Oldster Mobiles they degenerated into during the final years of badge-engineered blandness and Rental Car Specials.

In its heyday, the division offered high-class and Cadillac-level amenities in a more discreet package, along with a dash of exuberant performance comparable to Pontiacs. This winning combination helped make Oldsmobile one of the most appealing—and successful—brands of the 1960s and 1970s.

The Oldsmobile Vista Cruiser is arguably the *ur* wagon of the mid- to late Neolithic period in American automotive history. There were others, yes. But for Gen Xers born between the mid-1960s and early to mid-1970s, Oldsmobile's glorious nine-passenger

Oldsmobile distinguished its new-for-1964 station wagon by giving it a slick skylight over the rear passenger compartment. Though you really couldn't use these small windows for viewing any real vistas, they did give the Vista Cruiser a spacious, airy feel.

Left and above: **How about** a 4-4-2 station wagon equipped with a W-30 performance package? Station wagons don't get any cooler than this.

battle barge—with its signature multipaneled glass roof section—is an icon of their growing up years inextricably bound up with memories of *The Brady Bunch*, the Kiss Army, and bell-bottom corduroy Levis.

A mastodon like the Vista Cruiser as *family transpo* is almost not believable to those who didn't experience it firsthand. Not only was it rear-wheel drive (unlike virtually every modern family car, most notably the soul-killing minivan), it offered features and equipment no mewling minivan ever dared dream of—including heavy-duty manual transmissions and, of course, Oldsmobile's mighty Rocket V-8 engine.

Cup holders did *not* abound. Seat belts were few. Child safety seats nonexistent.

It was a marvelous moment in the life cycle of America. An era when mass and metal mattered more than crumple zones and traction control. A time before the Mom Movement—which spawned the minivan, among other things—gave us a culture that demands even eight-year-olds be cinched tightly into booster seats like miniature Hannibal Lecters instead of being permitted the joy of rolling around on the spacious and shag-carpeted floor of an avocado-green Vista Cruiser.

The Vista Cruiser came to life in 1964 as a wagonized version of the mid-size Cutlass and was actually second banana, size-wise, to the 88-based Dynamic wagon (as well as the later Delta 88–based Custom Cruiser). However, when the Dynamic 88 wagon was discontinued after the 1966 model year, the Vista became Oldsmobile's family truckster flagship and would become the best-known and longest remembered of the species.

As for the trademark Vista roof: It was reportedly inspired by the postwar Greyhound Scenicruiser bus—which had a Vista Dome glass roof over the rear two-thirds of its length. The idea was to afford riders a panoramic view of their surroundings and also to give the interior of the bus an airy, open feel. General Motors' GMC truck arm was also building the Scenicruiser buses in the 1950s and eventually the concept migrated to GM's passenger car studios.

You are looking at a car that is likely the only one of its kind.

Rocket Power, in the form of Oldsmobile's 330-cubic-inch V-8 (rated at 310 horsepower), was the early Vista Cruiser's first motive source. Many modern readers will be surprised to learn that in addition to its Jetaway two-speed (and later THM400 three-speed) automatic transmissions, Oldsmobile also offered both three- and four-speed *manual* transmissions (the latter "on the floor") in the Vista Cruiser, a feature as foreign to the mindset of the late-model minivan as giving the kiddies lawn darts for next season's Christmas presents.

Just imagine it: A *family wagon* with a 310-horsepower V-8, rear-wheel drive, *and* a clutch. Yes, you could get a limited slip axle, too. Just the ticket for towing a boat—or leaving a twin-patch Firestone tattoo on the pavement.

If you were a dad, it wasn't half-bad. And if you were a *teenager* borrowing Dad's ride, it was even *better*. In addition to its performance potential, there was room for half the football team—plus their dates and a keg.

GPS? iPod hookup? Music storage hard drive? No sir. In those days, the *car* kept you entertained. Distracting gadgets intended to make you forget about what a loser-mobile you were stuck with weren't necessary. The eight-track kept the Bee Gees humming—and if you needed company on a road trip, the Vista's optional Delco Remy CB radio was there for you.

In 1968, a second-generation Vista Cruiser made its debut. It rode on a new, longer 121-inch wheelbase, boasted 20 more standard cubic inches under the hood (350 Rocket V-8 in either 250-horsepower two-barrel or 310-horseppwer four-barrel versions) and offered all-new cosmetics based on the also-new and very handsome '68 Cutlass. The '68 Vista Cruiser was more fluid-looking, with gently bulging fenderwell arches pressed into the metal, an entirely new front end with vertical-slatted grille, and a smoother-looking bumper that appeared almost form-fitted to the nose rather than bolted-on, as it had looked on the previous generation. The rear bumper also tucked in gracefully—rising from the car's underside, with integrated bumperettes that rose on each side to meet up with the vertical taillights.

Another big change was to the design of the trademark Vista Roof. The main glass section was now a single piece, and the greenhouse effect was magnified by even larger sheets of side glass.

Luckily, in those days, freon was still the basis for AC systems, and GM was still using its industrial-scale Harrison compressors. Those things drew so much power to drive them that you could literally feel the engine stutter momentarily when you flipped on the AC and the compressor clutch engaged. *Nothing* frosted the vents like GM's freon-based Harrison AC systems of the 1960s and 1970s—even if it did cost you another couple of miles per gallon.

VISTA-CRUISER
All new from the top down!

Meet a brand new family-of-wagons for wagon families! Vista-Cruiser—a beautiful combination of prestige and practicality in four fashionable versions! Unique Vista-Roof gives you a whole new point of view! Lets you sit up, facing forward, even in three-seat models! Gives you extra room for cargo . . . and more height to load it. Add a spirited Jetfire Rocket V-8 that puts up to 290 horses to work for you. And a full ten-foot wheelbase to wed you to the road. Give it a try. You'll find a versatile new-size, you-size Oldsmobile Vista-Cruiser is your kind of wagon!

Longer 10-foot wheelbase cushions kids or cargo! Four deep-coil springs on a full ten-foot wheelbase give the Vista-Cruiser big-wagon ride and roadability even under a full load! Guard-Beam Frame, Twin-Triangle Stability help isolate noise and vibration.

Loading height makes Vista-Cruiser jack-of-all-trades! Wagon families are fast discovering the new versatility of the Vista-Cruiser. Higher loading height is ideal for upright delivery of merchandise, too. And Oldsmobile's winning style lends prestige on every trip!

Hidden storage compartment guards your treasures! Out of sight beneath the floor, this handy compartment provides extra storage space for valuables on all models. Measures 7.5 cubic feet on two-seat, 3.5 cubic feet on three-seat models. Lock is optional at extra cost.

But who cared? Gas—the real stuff, leaded regular—was well under a buck per gallon in the late 1960s.

Another cool Vista Cruiser touch was the dual-action tailgate, which folded out sideways as well as down. It could serve as an impromptu picnic table or perhaps as an additional riding platform in the days when no one thought twice about letting the kids sit there as Mom and Dad motored down a gravel road to the dock.

Also memorable were GM's power windows of the time, which zoomed up like mini guillotines and had no safety stops of any kind. Kids had to pay attention or let their fingers suffer the consequences. It was all good fun until Fido was decapitated.

Buyers could even equip their truckster in 442 trim—including both the 400-cube and (later, in 1970) 455-cube Rocket V-8s. With its high-flow Quadrajet four-barrel and dual exhausts, the 455 belted out 365 horsepower and tire-melting torque. The 442's dual-scooped, fiberglass, hood-pinned hood bolted right on, too.

Such equipment made highway trips memorable—and anyone who lived through

Unlike the other wagons in this chapter, the Oldsmobile Vista Cruiser was originally based on the division's mid-size chassis. It was still pretty fricking huge.

Vista Cruiser: Things to Know

The head of GM's Body Development Studio, Ray Koenig, gives credit for the Vista roof to stylist Pete Wozena.

The ultimate performance Vista Cruiser was briefly offered in 1972, when a handful of Hurst-modified versions were built. These cars featured a heavy-duty drivetrain, whose centerpiece was a high-performance Rocket 455 V-8.

Later Vista Cruisers (and Custom Cruisers) were sometimes powered by the Oldsmobile-built 403 V-8, an engine that was also used in some Pontiac Trans Ams beginning in 1979.

An Oldsmobile ad for the '69 Vista Cruiser featured George Plimpton and urged prospective buyers to consider a "youngmobile" like the Vista Cruiser.

The Vista Cruiser was actually slightly smaller than the Delta 88–based Custom Cruiser that first appeared in 1971 and ran through the early 1990s.

such an experience will never accept the wretched front-wheel-drive and traction-controlled substitutes foisted on the modern family.

The year 1972, unfortunately, would turn out to be the final year for the raised-panel Vista Roof. The 1973 restyle was probably motivated, at least in part, by roof crush standards that were being talked about in Washington. Though never implemented, these had a chilling effect on vehicle design—killing off most convertibles by the mid-1970s and forcing into the pages of automotive history such features as the Vista Roof.

Beginning with the '76 model year, the Vista Cruiser became plain old Cruiser, *sans* "Vista" in name as well as fact. From this point forward, the Delta 88–based Custom Cruiser would carry the flag. This was also the first year for square headlights—four of them, mounted side by side, with a single integrated turn-signal/parking lamp bar underneath each pair.

On the upside, the 455 (in tragically castrated form) stayed the course through 1976, and the Cruiser itself was still a most impressive land yacht. Its 114-inch wheelbase was down about half a foot, but this was nonetheless a big ride even in its time—and absolutely huge in ours. GM tried to retain at least the spirit of the Vista Roof, too, by designing a pop-up sunroof as an available feature.

But change was rustling in the air, and within a few years, even the memory of the Vista Cruiser would disappear into the morass of GM's ill-advised downsizing program—which culled real-wheel drive and V-8s in favor of unibodies, four cylinders, and front-wheel drive. The Vista Cruiser and Custom Cruiser gave way to the Ciera and Firenza wagons—pitiful little things that an Old School Vista Cruiser might have easily carried to the dump for recycling, thanks to its generous roof racks.

When Oldsmobile introduced the redesigned Vista Cruiser for the 1973 model year, the raised roof windows that defined the model from the beginning were absent. To put the "vista" in the cruiser and distinguish it from the standard Cutlass Supreme wagon, Oldsmobile gave the Vista Cruiser a sunroof.

BUICK'S
BATTLEWAGON
ESTATE WAGON
1970-1987

Presenting the totally-new 1970 Buick Estate Wagon.
With a totally-new approach to what a station wagon should look and drive like.
Because, above all, the 1970 Estate Wagon is a Buick. So it shares the sculpted Buick profile, the distinctive wide-angle grille. It looks as elegant and graceful as any Buick.
It drives like a Buick. Because, like all big Buicks, the 1970 Estate Wagon has AccuDrive, Buick's advance-design suspension system. Plus a special rear end suspension that's custom-designed for a station wagon's unique handling characteristics.
Like all Buicks, it has a cooling system that should never, ever overheat.

And a 455 cubic inch V-8, the largest smoothest V-8 ever made by Buick.
It's also standard on the 1970 Estate Wagon.
There's more. There's load space, lots of it. And it's backed by a two-way doorgate that makes loading anything or anybody that much easier. There's even a rear-facing third seat available at modest extra cost.
Best of all it's a Buick. With Buick quality and craftsmanship built right in.
And you know what that means.
The 1970 Buick Estate Wagon is something to believe in.

1970 BUICK ESTATE WAGON.
SOMETHING TO BELIEVE IN.

General Motors targeted the cars from its Buick division at people who wanted Cadillac-level luxury but didn't want to flaunt their wealth. Presumably even people who cranked out seven or more kids could still afford this level of luxury back then.

For the most fertile among the well-heeled, Buick offered a more luxurious spawn transporter—the Estate Wagon. Of the humongous seven- and nine-passenger station wagons built during the heyday of the Heavyweights, one of the standouts—and the longest to endure—was built by Buick.

Like the better-known Oldsmobile Vista Cruiser with which it shared a platform, the Estate Wagon was the minivan of the 1960s and 1970s. Two generations of kids grew up the *right* way—with carbureted V-8s and rear-wheel drive. Later, less fortunate generations would never know the magnificence of those days. Instead, their childhoods were spent strapped into booster seats in pitiful front-drive, four- and-six-cylinder K-car–derived shoeboxes full of safety devices but utterly devoid of personality.

They know not what they missed.

Some history: The name "Estate Wagon" dates back to the early 1940s, when Buick used it as a trim designation on the '40 Super, and later, for the Special and other wagonized versions of Buick's large sedans. Over the years, it was used to designate both a wagonized version of an existing model of sedan and of a separate model in its own right.

When World War II ended, Americans got busy rebuilding Europe. They also got busy on the home front, cranking out prodigious numbers of children. They needed large cars in which to haul all those kids, and the station wagon market boomed. Every automaker offered station wagons, including Buick.

Estate Wagon Interior Seating Appointments.

Beautiful...luxurious...and totally comfortable.
1. Elk-Grain-Expanded-Vinyl and Madrid-Grain Vinyl Notch Back Seats are available on the Two and Three Seat Estate Wagon in Green or Saddle. Sandalwood is available on the Three Seat Estate Wagon model only.
2. Elegant Elk-Grain and Madrid-Grain Vinyl Bench Seats are available on the Two and Three Seat Estate Wagon in Blue, Green, Sandalwood or Black. The new 1971 Estate Wagon control center enables the driver to almost instantly operate controls and see instruments and gauges at a glance. A comfortable fold-away forward facing rear bench seat is also available on some 1971 Estate Wagon models. Simply specify your interior trim selection when ordering from your Buick dealer.

Some of the equipment shown or described is available at extra cost.

Above: **Unlike many other** station wagons, which featured rear-facing jump seats that folded up from the storage area behind the passenger's seat, Buick's Estate Wagon featured front-facing third-row seats, a desirable feature for families with kids who suffered from carsickness.

Right: **When he needed** transportation to get out to his helicopter, the only obvious choice for any self-respecting rancher was Buick's opulent Estate Wagon.

Estate Wagon

Inside the Estate Wagons
Wider, more spacious. Increased load area. Stretch-out comfort surrounds you. The luxurious 1971 Buick 4-Door, Two and Three Seat Estate Wagons are truly something to believe in.

Two-Seat Model
Front head room: 39.6 inches; Rear head room: 39.3 inches; Front leg room: 42.6 inches; Rear leg room: 39.9 inches; Front shoulder room: 64.3 inches; Rear shoulder room: 63.3 inches.

Three-Seat Model
Front head room: 39.6 inches; Rear head room: 39.4 inches; Front leg room: 42.6 inches; Rear leg room: 37.9 inches; Front shoulder room: 64.3 inches; Rear shoulder room: 63.3 inches.

Outside the Estate Wagon
A longer, lower silhouette. Distinctive new grill. Sculpted beauty in every graceful line. The 1971 Buick 4-Door, Two and Three Seat Estate Wagons share the same exterior dimensions: Length: 226.8 inches; Width: 79.7 inches; Height: 57.3 inches; Wheelbase: 127.0 inches. (Note: Estate Wagon interior and exterior dimensions are approximations in inches.)

Estate Wagon Performance
Responsive. Eager. Performance to believe in.
Standard engine: 455-4 V8; Compression ratio: 8.5:1; Displacement: 455 C.I.D.; Carburetion: 4-barrel.

Transmission: Standard: 3-speed manual (column shift) Turbo Hydra-matic 400 Automatic Transmission.
Rear Axle Ratio: 3-speed manual: 3.42; automatic: 2.93. Consult your Buick dealer for information on available ratios.

Estate Wagon Comfort
Gracious convenience where it counts. New innovations where they matter. Estate Wagon is a state of comfort. New Full-Flo ventilation system, heater and defroster; front door-operated interior light; glove compartment light; smoking set; front and rear seat ash trays; Magic-Mirror exterior finish; arm rests; front and rear deep pile carpeting; custom interior trims; full-foam seats in addition to many other comfort features your Buick dealer will be pleased to discuss with you.

Estate Wagon Special Features
Special in every respect. Special with Estate Wagon for your very special enjoyment. variable ratio power steering; 6,000 mile lubed front suspension; L78 x 15 bias belted tires; direct-acting hydraulic shock absorbers, front and rear; self-adjusting power front disc brakes with composite cast iron rear drum brakes; Buick's AccuDrive with forward mounted steering gear and linkage; Delcotron generator; Full-Flow oil filter; right and left outside rear view mirrors; four-way hazard warning flasher; radio antenna concealed in the windshield; side guard beam construction for added protection; safety door latches and hinges; padded energy absorbing instrument panel; newly designed instrument cluster for easier serviceability; semi-closed cooling system that should never overheat, even with air conditioning; foam padded front head restraints; anti-theft key warning buzzer; anti-theft steering column lock; time modulated carburetor choke control for jet starts in any weather; four jet windshield washers; new evaporative emission control system.

Some of the equipment shown or described is available at extra cost.

The Buick Estate Wagon.

These jumbo-size family movers grew to their full magnificence during the early 1970s. By the 1970 model year, the Estate Wagon's wheelbase was a very solid 124 inches—still not quite up to the fulsome 127 inches of the 225 sedan, but respectable. This would grow 3 more inches the following year, to 127 inches—and dead even with the hulking "deuce and quarter."

Early models featured woodie side panels and G's famous clamshell flip-out/flip-down tailgate system that survived well into the 1970s. Base models had twin-bench seating, but an optional third row could be specified.

Sportwagon versions shared the iconic raised roof section with glass side panels also offered on Oldsmobile's Vista Cruiser. Those fortunate enough to have grown up with an Estate Wagon will have fond memories of bouncing around like so much unsecured flotsam and jetsam in the expansive cargo area—Mom and Dad distant presences, far away, up front. There were no mandatory child restraint laws in those days—and seat belts were definitely *optional*.

Most of the big lunkers from the early to mid–disco era also came standard with Buick's mountain motor, the 7.4-liter 455 working through a heavy-duty three-speed Turbo-Hydramatic. Teenagers quickly learned the trick of flipping over the air cleaner lid to let the huge Quadrajet four-barrel carb breathe easier, its banshee wail reaching full-throat fury as the secondaries opened up. Power-braking the big V-8-powered behemoth roasted the whitewall tires out back, which disappeared in a haze of blue smoke, molten bits of rubber glazed on the lower rear quarters the only evidence of many a 16-year-old's first experience of "high performance."

Unfortunately, as the 1970s progressed, big engines began to disappear—even though cars like the still-large Estate Wagon very much required their services. The final year for the 455 was 1976. All Buick V-8s (including the small-bore 350) would be discontinued shortly thereafter. Beginning with the 1980 models, the biggest gun available was an Oldsmobile-sourced 5.0-liter 307-cubic-inch V-8 that struggled under the yoke of the Estate Wagon's curb weight.

The end for the Estate Wagon is somewhat indeterminate. The final year for the "old" style—and for the rear-drive Estate Wagon as a distinct model within Buick's model lineup—was 1990. This was also the last year an Estate Wagon left the factory, equipped with the Oldsmobile-sourced 307 V-8, detuned to 140 horsepower.

However, a larger, rear-drive Buick wagon returned in the early 1990s; this was a wagonized version of the new Roadmaster, which was a Buick-trimmed version of the new Chevy Impala, a car that was sometimes derisively referred to as Shamu because of its rounded whale-like girth.

Both cars shared the same corporate (Chevy-built) drivetrains based on the Corvette's 5.7-liter 350-cubic-inch V-8. So even though Buick identified its version as the Buick Roadmaster Estate Wagon, which ran through 1996, it was, at best, a faint echo of the full-blooded versions that preceded it.

Buick kept the rear-drive Estate Wagon in its lineup long after its sedans had switched to front-wheel drive.

Estate Wagon: Things to Know

Decades before GMC used the name for its version of the Chevy El Camino, Buick sold an Estate Wagon Caballero. This model was offered by Buick for only two model years, from 1957 to 1958.

Most of the 1970s-era Estate Wagons were built at the plant in Arlington, Texas, which was given the production of pickups and SUVs after GM cancelled the last of its large, rear-wheel-drive sedans and wagons in the mid-1990s.

The 1980 Estate Wagon was the first Estate Wagon to carry an MSRP higher than $10,000 ($10,806).

The 1953 Estate Wagon was the last woodie wagon to use real wood exterior body panels. Subsequent models had all-steel bodies.

By the 1980s, the Estate Wagon (and its "twins" within GM) was one of just two full-size, rear-drive, V-8 wagons still in production. The other was Ford's Country Squire, which Ford cancelled after 1991, leaving the Roadmaster Estate Wagon to soldier on by itself until 1996.

FATTIE FORD
LTD COUNTRY SQUIRE
1969-1991

FORD · TORINO/FAIRLANE · FALCON · CLUB WAGON · BRONCO

When it came to its Country Squire wagons, Ford didn't mess around. These were full-size family transport units from day one.

Part of the reason Ford is currently the strongest U.S. automaker may be due to luck and partly due to better management. But Ford did one thing its rivals failed to do that might prove more determinative in the final analysis. And that is simply that Ford stuck to its guns—including its V-8 and rear-wheel-drive guns—more steadfastly and longer than either GM or Chrysler. It specifically continued to build traditional family trucksters for years after Chrysler threw in the towel and went with K-cars so small they could have been sold as prizes in boxes of Cracker Jack. And GM frittered away the legacy (as well as annual sales figures) of storied nameplates like Oldsmobile, Buick, and Pontiac.

Though eventually even Ford knuckled under and joined the downsized front-wheel-drive Dark Side, it survives to this day in great measure because of the lingering greatness of its American-size rear-drive and V-8-powered dreadnoughts.

The Era of the Big Wagons, roughly from the early 1950s through the late 1980s—was less hectic than modern times. Most families lived comfortably on one income. Mom was usually home if there were kids in the house. Going for a Sunday drive was a popular form of recreation. And for many of those long-gone American families, the car of choice was the majestic Ford Country Squire.

Three things made it special.

First, it was always a heavy roller. Unlike other brands of wagon, Ford never made a small or even mid-size Country Squire. Over its entire model run, the wood-paneled wonder never had anything less substantial than the underthings of Ford's largest sedan, stretched if need be to accommodate a full-size American family.

Where others put the name of a once-impressive wagon on a lesser car and hoped no one would notice, Ford always made sure the Country Squire Crest was never degraded in this manner. Whether the chassis underneath derived from a Custom DeLuxe, Crestline, Fairlane, Galaxie, LTD, or Crown Vic, it was always the biggest thing in Ford's inventory—and always full-frame and rear-wheel drive, with a V-8 engine under the hood, too.

Second, in the Ford hierarchy, Country Squire meant top-of-the-line. These wagons were never Blue Light Specials, unlike some of the lower-trimmed wagons purveyed by others. Not that there's anything wrong with low-cost, of course, but if you wanted something truly splendid, Country Squire was your chariot.

Like other broad-in-the-beam wagons of the 1960s and 1970s, the Country Squire could take nine passengers in three rows of seats. And like other wagons of that period,

the automakers were still largely free to try out ideas before lawsuit fear and the endless regulation of federal safety nags put the kybosh on innovation. In today's world, options such as available sideways-facing (and fold-down) third-row seats would never see the light of day.

Third, every Country Squire came with wood-paneled flanks, from the original 1950 model all the way to the final 1991 model. Early 1950s models used *real* wood, too.

The year 1954 would be the first year for all-steel bodies, which were more practical to build and far less maintenance-intensive for the owner. But the *woodie* look would continue for another 40 years—and be emulated by GM and Chrysler—via fiberglass "wood" trimmed panels (your choice of birch or maple finish) that were fitted to the metal side panels.

The Country Squire name dates back to the 1950 model year, when a new two-door wagon appeared to replace the former Custom wagon. Ford positioned the new model near the top of its food chain. The name was intended to summon forth notions of landed country gentry, a sort of Americanized version of what the English call a "shooting brake" only on a much grander scale.

First-year base price was $2,028 with the buyer's choice of a 95-horsepower inline six (226 cubic inches) or 100-horsepower flathead V-8 (239 cubic inches).

Ford marketing called it the "Double Duty Dandy," noting that it could carry eight people thanks to its innovative "Stowaway" center seat and "Flat Deck" cargo area. With the tailgate down, the deck stretched nearly 10 feet long—nearly *4 feet* longer than a late-model pickup's standard six-foot bed. It also featured high-grade vinyl and simulated leather interior trim as well as the new Ford-O-Matic two-speed automatic transmission.

Base price was about $300 to $500 more than a sedan or coupe, a not-small jump that made it the most expensive Ford model available that year. The Country Squire's sticker price was even higher than the convertible coupe, which carried an MSRP of $1,948.

The wheelbase, which began at a relatively restrained 114 inches, shot upward as the years passed, and the big Fords that provided the wagon's underpinnings grew bigger. By 1959, it was up to 118 inches—sharing its basic platform with the new Galaxie (and Mercury Monterey).

Like its full-sized sedans, Ford offered the Country Squire wagon in several trim levels, culminating in the LTD versions.

The mid-1970s Ford Country Squire wagon was as honest as it could be, design-wise; it was a large box on wheels that didn't pretend to look like anything other than a large box on wheels.

Ten years later, in 1969, the Country Squire rode on the LTD's stately 121-inch wheelbase—which would last all the way through to 1978.

And yet, despite the girth of these wood-paneled plesiosaurs, they always managed to look good. The 1967 to 1968 models, for example, had the same attractive forward-canted, front-end, and vertical-stacked quad headlights as the same-year Galaxie coupe and sedan, giving the big wagon a sporty countenance. The restyled 1969s to 1972s, meanwhile, had the LTD's stately-looking, hidden headlights and subtle hood pleats.

It was always classy, never clumsy.

Some of the automotive industry's most enormous V-8s powered the Country Squire, too, including a 460-cubic-inch monster (beginning in 1973) that outclassed even the gigantic 454 big-block used in competitors like the Chevy Kingswood. It's true the 460 drank gas like the Exxon *Valdez* leaked crude and barely produced more than 200 net horsepower in mid-1970s tune, but it had the endless reserves of low-rpm torque necessary to get 4,629 pounds of Ford wagon moving, and that was all that really mattered.

Even though the wagon's sails were trimmed a bit beginning with the 1979 models, wheelbase still stood at 114.3 inches, which was slightly more than the original 1950 model, and by this time, bigger than almost anything else on the road. Overall length was 216 inches—impressive by any standard.

Ford hung tough all the way through to 1991, too, continuing to offer a full-size (Crown Victoria–based) Country Squire wagon even after most of its competitors had fallen by the wayside or been downsized into front-wheel-drive desperation.

Eventually, even Ford had to give up on the Old School wagon, which had become a stranger in a strange land by the early 1990s. People cared about fuel economy now, and the government cared about safety. Though two-ton wagons have the inherent advantage of mass on their side, the things that made traditional wagons special, like those ambulance-style, sideways-mounted third seats, had become as politically incorrect as catalytic converter "test pipes." The Squire had to be retired. In 1992, Ford replaced it with a wagon version of the Taurus sedan. It sold extremely well and made Ford a pile of money.

But for those of a certain age, it just wasn't the same anymore.

Ford stuck to its guns, keeping the Country Squire large while other automakers downsized their station wagons.

Country Squire: Things to Know

Reportedly, Gordon Buehrig, legendary stylist of Auburns and Cords in the 1930s, contributed to the design of the early '50s Country Squire.

Ford marketed the Country Squire's two-piece tailgate as the "Magic Door." It had a retractable (manual or electric) glass upper section and a fold-flat lower gate.

A factory option on Country Squires equipped with the sideways-facing third row was a collapsible checkers table with magnetically attached playing pieces.

The "Family Truckster" used in the *National Lampoon Vacation* series was based on a mid-'70s Country Squire.

Ford used the "Squire" name to designate high-trim versions of other cars, including the compact Pinto wagon. But a Country Squire was always a Country Squire and based on a full-size Ford.

The Country Squire stayed in Ford's product line until 1991, when the Crown Victoria upon which the wagon was based was given a modern aerodynamic redesign. At that point the Crown Victory Country Squire abdicated its crown to the Taurus wagon.

PAUNCHY PONTIAC
SAFARI
1957–1989

STAR CHIEF CUSTOM SAFARI

TWO-DOOR CHIEFTAIN SAFARI

*Load up and light out
for adventure . . .*

There's no better way than in one of these beautiful, spacious Star Flight styled Safaris. At the wheel you enjoy all the handling ease, riding comfort and smooth-flowing power of America's Number One Road Car plus the convenience of space for up to nine passengers or a half-ton load. You have four Safari models to choose from in a variety of nineteen solid and two-tone color combinations in the Star Chief Safari—sixty-eight in the Super Chief and Chieftain.

THE *Safari* SERIES

AMERICA'S NUMBER 1 ROAD CAR

SUPER CHIEF SAFARI

FOUR-DOOR CHIEFTAIN SAFARI

Originally, Pontiac's Safari station wagon was a two-door model, a sister to Chevrolet's Nomad. In 1959, the name was applied to Pontiac's four-door station wagons as well.

GM's Pontiac division was sent off on its own version of the Trail of Tears in 2009—after years of broken treaties and forked tongue-talking with the corporation's upper management.

Part of the reason for the decline and fall of Pontiac can be traced to the loss of the division's formerly unique, Pontiac-built powertrains, a process that began in the early 1980s when the last of the Pontiac-designed V-8s (the 301) was killed off, and subsequent models with V-8 engines were fitted with corporate engines built (mostly) by Chevrolet. The second unkind cut was the forced homogenization of Pontiac's model lineup, which became (for the most part) little more than tarted-up and rebadged Chevys and Buicks.

The Safari wagon wasn't like that—while it was allowed to live, anyhow.

The first model appeared in 1955 as a custom-bodied two-door wagonized version of the Star Chief, riding on a stately 124-inch wheelbase.

Though it shared some basic metalwork with the Chevy Nomad, the Safari had a unique two-door shell as well as numerous unique design flourishes, including a beautiful front-end treatment with an ornate, multisection bumper. The oval main

THE ADVENTURE-LOVING
SAFARI

adds a thrilling new dimension to driving!

The station wagon way of life is here to stay—and nothing makes it more easygoing, more fun, more comfortable than a big, nimble, responsive Pontiac Safari. Shown here is the regal six-passenger, 2-seat Bonneville, with fully retractable, roll-down rear window. Pontiac's Wide-Track Wheels and big 122" wheelbase cradle you in town-car comfort wherever the trail leads—and the Bonneville Safari's four-barrel, 300-h.p. (with Hydra-Matic) Tempest V-8 makes light work of any load or road. In short—wherever this spirited Bonneville urges you, admiring glances will be a steady reminder that you're driving the ultimate in wagons.

Here's exclusive BONNEVILLE beauty that will last and last in durable Morrokide. Shown here are Jeweltone Medium Green and Pale Green Morrokide with Dark Green Morrokide accent. Other colors: 3-Tone Blue, Ivory-Maroon-Mahogany and Beige-Copper-Mahogany.

BONNEVILLE CUSTOM SAFARI

Pontiac's Safari wagon benefited from the division's "wide-track" design, created by moving the wheels out toward the edge of the chassis. Pontiac developed this design not because of its inherent stability, as the division's advertisements suggested, but rather because division chairman Bunkie Knudsen thought the narrow-wheelbase cars looked like "football players wearing ballet slippers."

Below: **Then, as now,** station wagons weren't exactly the coolest cars on the road. Pontiac emphasized the stylishness and sportiness of the Safari wagon rather than focusing on its more utilitarian aspects, like the sheer quantity of people it could haul.

BONNEVILLE CUSTOM SAFARI

Safari

Whatever you want in a station wagon—you get it in extra measure in a Pontiac Safari.

Elegance? Choose the Bonneville Custom Safari and enjoy exclusive Bonneville luxury including deep loop pile carpeting throughout and matchless interiors.

Utility with luxury? Then select a Catalina Safari— 6- or 9-passenger. In both models all but the front seat fold flush with the floor. Rear window is retractable—crank-operated on the 6-passenger (power-operated optional). Power operation is standard on the 9-passenger.

Isn't it time to step up your motoring pleasure with a Safari? The whole family will enjoy the fun.

Bonneville Custom Safari upholstery includes genuine pleats in Jeweltone Morrokide, aerated for added comfort. Three tri tone color combinations. Deep loop pile wall-to-wall carpeting with stainless steel protective skid strips in load area. Catalina Safaris offer five Jeweltone Morrokide three-tone color choices, with combination loop pile carpeting and vinyl surfaced rubber floor covering in passenger areas. Catalina load floors are embossed vinyl mat.

Left and above: **From the very first** Safari wagon, Pontiac sought to offer growing families child-conveyance devices with style. (Left in Bonneville trim.)

section was set behind a pair of bumperettes on either side, with vertical sections forming a cross at each end. The amount of chrome used was impressive even then, and unimaginable in our time, when the caustic chrome-plating process has become as environmentally verboten as pouring used motor oil into a storm sewer.

Twin bands running the length of the hood, a forward-canted B-pillar, and traditional "chief" styling icons further differentiated the Safari from other GM models on the outside. On the inside, the Safari boasted sliding (rather than fixed or push-out) glass for the rear windows; while under the hood, Pontiac's own 287 V-8 gave the big wagon a special war whoop. The 287 was making as much as 200 horsepower in 1955—more power than the just-launched (and more famous) Chevy small-block that appeared that same year.

In 1957, the Safari was offered in both two- and four-door forms—the Safari Transcontinental. It could seat nine and was loaded with extra trim and an upgraded interior, with a punched-out 347 V-8 under the hood. By this time, the Pontiac V-8 was producing as much as 290 horsepower (compared with the same year Chevy 283, which maxed out at 283 *with fuel injection*), making it one of the most potent "small" engines of its time.

Unfortunately, whether because of ineffective marketing or its higher price tag (more than $3,000 in 1957 when a Low Budget Special Chevy Beauville wagon sold for about

Pontiac offered Safari wagons based on the full-size sedans as well as the intermediate-size LeMans sedan.

The full-size station wagons built by General Motors in the 1970s were some of the most versatile vehicles ever offered to the public. They still are.

Country Squire: Things to Know

Though never offered with a wood body, the Safari was available with simulated wood appliqué along its flanks.

Safaris of the early 1970s shared the famous clamshell dual-opening rear gate used on other GM wagons of the period.

Performance-oriented features, such as 15×7 Rally wheels, were common upgrades found on mid-'70s Safaris. It has been rumored that a few of Pontiac's HO 455 V-8s may have found their way into a handful of early '70s Safaris.

Pontiac V-8s ranged in displacement from 287 to 455 cubic inches, but there were never big- or small-blocks. Externally, all Pontiac V-8s are largely identical, with differences in displacement achieved by different bore/stroke combinations.

The heaviest Safari was the '74 nine-passenger model with 455 V-8. It weighed 5,112 pounds without passengers on board.

SAFARI 2-SEAT STATION WAGON

SAFARI 3-SEAT STATION WAGON

$2,500 and a Nomad cost under $2,800), the Safari never caught on. During its first three years on the market, fewer than 15,000 Safari wagons found homes. This was considerably below the one-year sales performance of the Nomad wagon, which sold more than 20,000 copies in 1957.

In subsequent years, the Safari would be based on the full-size Bonneville sedan and offered in both six- and nine-passenger forms—though henceforth always with four doors. Though it lost some of its aesthetic individuality throughout the 1960s and 1970s, the Safari continued to offer pure Pontiac power under the hood, including the legendary 389/421—and eventually, 455— V-8 engines. Safari became Grand Safari in 1971, rolling on a truly Herculean 127-inch wheelbase, which was even longer than the Bonneville's. This biggest of all Safaris ran through the 1976 model year, before GM's company-wide downsizing program chopped nearly a foot off the big wagon's wheelbase. By 1982, the wheelbase had been reduced to a Camaro-size 108.1 inches and curb weight reduced by nearly 700 pounds. Big wagons were on the way out—at Pontiac and elsewhere.

The final Safari was bolted together in 1989, one of just 5,146 to leave the factory that year.

LeMans Safaris

Pontiac's mid-sized station wagons.

1980 Grand LeMans Safari.
The efficiency of a mid-size
with a full-measure of luxury.

Pontiac doesn't call Grand
LeMans Safari grand for
nothing. Shown with available
60/40 notchback cloth seating.

30

When Pontiac introduced the LeMans Safari, the full-size Safari was renamed the Grand Safari.

From 1982 onward the Safari was only available in shrunken form; the Grand Safari was history.

AFTERWORD
LUSTING FOR LARD?

While the book you just finished reading is mostly a funeral dirge for a type of car that will never be made in mass quantities ever again, there *is* an upside to the situation: Unlike Corvettes, name-brand muscle cars, and other high-profile collectibles, most of the cars featured in this book are—for now—very affordable. Many are cheap enough that you can buy on a whim, shelling out little more than you'd spend to acquire a fairly bedraggled used Corolla.

Let me give you an example.

As I was finishing up this book, I came across a local ad for a '75 Cadillac Fleetwood Brougham. It was a one-owner car, with the original title from 1975. As is common with these cars, it was owned by an older gentleman who, for the past 20-plus years, rarely drove it and when he did drove it gently. Mostly, it just sat.

Cars like this—the excessive sedans and plus-size coupes you've been reading about—tend not to have been modified by idiot teenagers or treated like 45-year-old ladies of the night in a backstreet Tijuana brothel. This old Caddy still had its original GM pellet-style catalytic converter (1975 was the first year). Almost all its paint—bronze chocolate metallic—was untouched, and the spare had never been down. A bit over 70,000 miles. *Asking* price?

$3,900.

I have no doubt the Brougham could have been mine for $3,500 or so—about what you'd pay for a well-used economy car with 200,000 miles on the clock. You cannot touch a classic-era Camaro or Mustang for this kind of money. You *might* get a decent parts/project car—maybe (if you are really lucky) a tired driver that will start and move (sort of) under its own power.

But here was a nice old road hog—a living piece of Americana—that promised fun as big as its eight-liter V-8 for almost pocket change, the kind of money you'd spend on a decent riding lawn mower.

This is not uncommon.

Big old cars are (for now) almost unbelievably inexpensive. Remember—they were not considered hot commodities when new; the hot rod crowd isn't interested in them and (so far) the collector car hobby has not deigned to notice them. Thus, the acquisition costs are not ridiculous—as they have become if you want, say, a big-block Charger.

Insurance and the cost of keeping these cars in good operating condition are generally cheap, too. Most are powered by the same basic engines and have the same basic guts underneath as popular models, so obtaining things like air and oil filters, gaskets, etc., is as easy as heading over to your nearest NAPA store.

There are, in sum, few ways to have as much fun dabbling in the vintage car market for so little investment. It is much easier on the budget—and family life—to toss three or four grand at a dry-docked dreadnought like the '75 Brougham than it is to rationalize sinking $50K into a 340 Six Pak AAR 'Cuda.

America's Number ① Road Car...

And unlike that $50K 'Cuda—which you'd be afraid to drive for fear of getting hit, or even stone-chipped—you can take your old tank anywhere short of downtown Detroit. Own a high-dollar classic and your garage becomes a target for thieves—and you will become as paranoid about security as someone with a duffel bag filled with $100,000 in the hall closet.

This, too, takes away from the fun of owning a mainline classic.

But with something that's cheap to buy, not yet the focus of speculator greedheads, and not yet in anyone's gunsights (except perhaps the smog police), you can relax and enjoy your new toy in a way that the owner of a 427 Corvette will never be able to do.

Also, you will be driving something different—a real conversation piece, something no one else has brought to the show. Instead of being one of 15 early Trans Ams sitting side by side, there you will be with your (probably) one-of-a-kind (or at least, one-of-a-kind in your county) Electra 225s—or Caddy Fleetwood.

Maybe you'll be lucky enough to have a *d'Elegance* model, even!

Naturally there are some downsides. Let's start with the elephant in the room—literally. Size. The cars lovingly caressed in this book are absolutely enormous. You have no concept of this until you come face to face with one. The reason I did not buy the '75 Fleetwood was that it was about 20 feet from the edge of its massive jowl of a bumper to the jutting tips of its twin tail fins—and would literally have eaten up almost all of the available square footage in my *oversize* garage. And keep in mind that most homes built after the 1980s do *not* have oversize garages. They were built with modern (read, much smaller) cars in mind. Even a large SUV—though heavy and tall—is nowhere near as *long* and *wide* through the hips as a stretched out '75 Caddy, or similar beast. So: Measure before you buy. Be *sure* it will fit—because odds are it may not. Needless to say, this also goes for parking spots (good luck), narrow bridges, and everywhere else built years after the last plus-size roller was sent off to automotive Elba.

Next, the actual driving part.

People currently in their 40s and older will probably have had some previous experience —in their teens and 20s—with *Americanus gigantosaurus.* If Mom and Dad didn't have one when they were growing up, Grandma and Grandpa likely did. Maybe you learned to drive in one (like me). If so, you will know about the heaving, Sta-Puff shocks—the overboosted, disconnected steering with less feel for the road than George W. Bush has for English grammar. The way the rear brakes lock up when you try to stop suddenly—the back end often coming around to say hello.

So, be careful. Especially your first time out. Take it easy, just like you would if someone on the bridge of the Missouri handed you the tiller and asked you to parallel park it.

The rest, as they say, is gravy.

Enjoy!

In the 1950s, and even into the 1960s, auto manufacturers offered accessory kits that relocated spare tires to the rear bumpers. These so-called "Continental kits" raised havoc with a vehicle's weight distribution, but on such oversized vehicles that was of little consequence. What did matter was that the owners were stylin'.

INDEX